ARCTIC

FOREST

NORTHEAST WOODLANDS

NORTH ATLANTIC COAST

GREAT LAKES

MERICAN

PRAIRIE

APPALACHIAN HIGHLANDS

SOUTH ATLANTIC COAST AND PIEDMONT

SOUTHERN HILL COUNTRY

GULF COAST

Stories from Where We Live

The Great Lakes

The *Stories from Where We Live* Series

Each volume in the *Stories from Where We Live* series celebrates a North American ecoregion through its own distinctive literature. For thousands of years, people have told stories to convey their community's cultural and natural history. *Stories from Where We Live* reinvigorates that tradition in hopes of helping young people better understand the place where they live. The anthologies feature poems, stories, and essays from historical and contemporary authors, as well as from the oral traditions of each region's indigenous peoples. Together they document the geographic richness of the continent and reflect the myriad ways that people interact with and respond to the natural world. We hope that these stories kindle readers' imaginations and inspire them to explore, observe, ponder, and protect the place they call home.

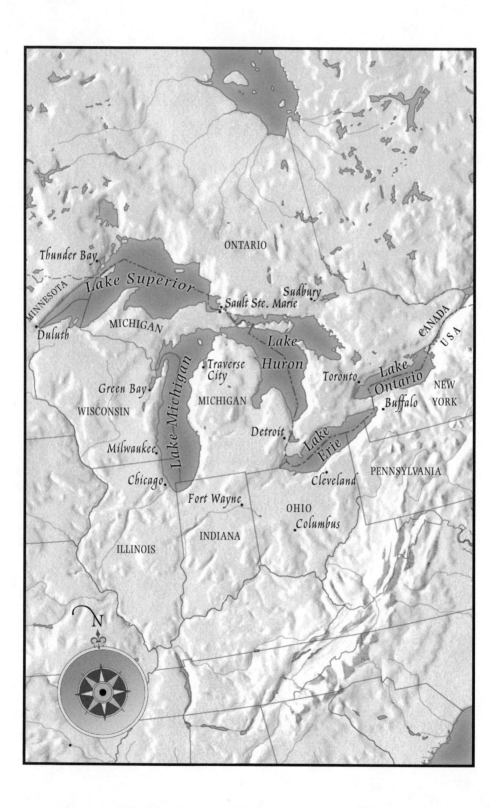

Stories from Where We Live

The Great Lakes

EDITED BY SARA ST. ANTOINE

Maps by Paul Mirocha
Illustrations by Trudy Nicholson

MILKWEED EDITIONS

Published 2003 by Milkweed Editions
Printed in Canada
Jacket design by Paul Mirocha
Jacket and interior illustrations by Trudy Nicholson
Jacket and interior maps by Paul Mirocha
Interior design by Wendy Holdman
The text of this book is set in Legacy.
03 04 05 06 07   5 4 3 2 1
First Edition

Special underwriting for this book was provided in honor of Wallace C. Dayton.

Milkweed Editions, a nonprofit publisher, gratefully acknowledges support from the Bush
Foundation; Joe B. Foster Family Foundation; Furthermore, a program of the J. M. Kaplan
Fund; General Mills Foundation; Jerome Foundation; Dorothy Kaplan Light; Lila Wallace-
Reader's Digest Fund; Marshall Field's Project Imagine with support from the Target
Foundation; McKnight Foundation; Minnesota State Arts Board through an appropriation
by the Minnesota State Legislature; National Endowment for the Arts; Kate and Stuart
Nielsen; Deborah Reynolds; St. Paul Companies, Inc.; Ellen and Sheldon Sturgis; Surdna
Foundation; Target Foundation; Gertrude Sexton Thompson Charitable Trust; James R.
Thorpe Foundation; Toro Foundation; United Arts Fund of COMPAS; Lois Ream Waldref;
Brenda Wehle and John C. Lynch; and Xcel Energy Foundation.

Library of Congress Cataloging-in-Publication Data

Stories from where we live—The Great Lakes / edited by Sara St. Antoine ; maps by Paul
    Mirocha ; illustrations by Trudy Nicholson.
        p. cm.—(Stories from where we live)
    ISBN 1-57131-639-6 (cloth)
        1. American literature—Great Lakes Region. 2. Great Lakes Region—Literary collec-
    tions. 3. Great Lakes—Literary collections. 4. Great Lakes Region. 5. Great Lakes
    I. St. Antoine, Sara, 1966- II. Nicholson, Trudy H. III. Series.

    PS561 .S76 2002
    810.8'077—dc21

                                                                    2002071837

This book is printed on acid-free paper.

Stories from Where We Live
The Great Lakes

Great Places

Reapers and Sowers

Wild Lives

Appendixes: Ecology of the Great Lakes

An Invitation

Ever since human communities first formed in the Great Lakes region, people have been describing, celebrating, and making sense of their home through stories.

Native peoples living around Lake Erie and Lake Ontario believed the roar of Niagara Falls was the voice of the Great Spirit of the waters.

Peoples farther west claimed that Michigan's Sleeping Bear Dunes formed when a mother bear lay down to rest after swimming across Lake Michigan to escape a Wisconsin forest fire.

According to Iroquois legend, the yellow lady slippers that grow in the region's woods are moccasins created for a young girl who gave hers away to an injured whippoorwill.

Today, we still tell these and other stories to help us understand and honor the place where we live. In this anthology, we've collected some of this literature—poems, essays, short stories, and journal entries that portray the rich natural and cultural history of the Great Lakes region. Each of these writings comes to us from someone who has called the region home, from early Ojibwe storytellers to turn-of-century botanists to contemporary city residents. Through their works, these authors offer us windows into the life and landscapes of the Great Lakes region.

The ecoregion as we have defined it includes the five Great

Lakes—Superior, Michigan, Huron, Ontario, and Erie—as well as the lands around them. It stretches across all of Michigan and parts of Minnesota, Wisconsin, Illinois, Indiana, Ohio, Pennsylvania, New York, and Ontario.

If you walked the perimeter of the region, you would of course encounter abundant lakes, great and small, at every turn. You might also notice some marked changes in the countryside over the course of your journey. That's because the Great Lakes region lies at a fascinating biological crossroads, where the leafy woodlands of the Northeast meet the prairies of the Midwest and the needle-leaf forests of the far North. The result is a great variety of habitats that together support an unusual roster of regional wildlife, from meadowlarks to white-tailed deer to moose and loons. Of course, not all of this region is wild habitat. Large portions now comprise farms, mid-sized towns, and major industrial cities, including Milwaukee, Chicago, Detroit, Cleveland, and Toronto. But even in these human-dominated places, one can find traces of the plant and animal communities that once flourished more widely.

Immerse yourself in the literature of this anthology and you'll get a better sense of the region's people, places, and wildlife. You'll read about the daring of sailors and sledders in "Adventures." You'll explore dunes, rivers, lakes, and woodlands in "Great Places." In "Reapers and Sowers" you'll discover some of the many ways that people depend on and care for local resources. And in "Wild Lives" you'll get closer to the region's many animals—the bears and wolves that prowl the northern wilderness, and the squirrels and raccoons that scratch out a living in backyards and alleyways.

We hope this anthology leaves you more knowledgeable and curious about the Great Lakes region, whether it's a place you hope to visit or the place you now call home. With luck, we'll be hearing some of your own Great Lakes stories in the months and years to come.

—Sara St. Antoine

Stories from Where We Live

The Great Lakes

Adventures

We Are the Early Risers

JoAnn Early Macken

We are the early risers.
We are drawn to the water
like turtles in spring.
While the sleepyheads snuggle with pillows,
we are shucking off sneakers and socks
to tiptoe through sand dunes
and wade in the shallows
and watch dawn hatch from the waves.

JoAnn Early Macken *is the author of two rhyming picture books,* Sing-Along Song *and* Cats on Judy, *and four series of nonfiction books for beginning readers. She teaches children to write poetry, and her poems have appeared in several children's magazines. A graduate of the M.F.A. in Writing for Children and Young Adults program at Vermont College, she lives in Wisconsin with her husband and their two sons.*

Fairies' Washing

APRIL PULLEY SAYRE

The thrill of exploring a place you know well at an unusual time of day can be just as great as—maybe even greater than—exploring altogether new terrain. You may be surprised to see how much the natural world remakes itself as the hours of the days go by.

I always knew Nanna got up early in the mornings. Once, I asked my father why.

"Older people like your Nanna don't need as much sleep as I do," he said with a drawn-out yawn.

But that wasn't the reason she got up so early. That wasn't the reason at all.

"Only early risers can see the jewel bird awake," she would say as she climbed the stairs to bed. Mom, Dad, and I, we laughed. We played cards until the wee, late hours of night.

But then, one Saturday, I woke up early, in that blue, inky light before dawn. Nanna, her flowered robe wrapped tortilla tight, was creeping by my bedroom door.

Where was she going? I wanted to know.

So I grabbed my clothes and followed her on tiptoed feet: first into the kitchen, then out the door into the yard.

Cold air forced my eyes wide open.

"Who-cooks for you?" called the last owl of the night.

Nanna disappeared into the woods.

I worried that Nanna might fall in the dark, tangled woods. But I was the one who tripped and fell.

"Be quiet and listen," she ordered, sounding stern.

I did, and heard echoes and eerie sounds. They were strange, wet whistles, like songs sung in a cave.

"Dawn songs," explained Nanna. "Birds sing them only at dawn."

I listened a while longer. But then I had to ask. "Where are you going so early?"

"To see the jewel bird," she said, and pushed aside a branch. It snapped back, splattering water on my shirt. When I looked up again, she was gone.

Dad had told me Nanna made up the jewel bird. But what if he was wrong?

I ran to catch her, but she was fast. Branches and leaves slapped my arms and legs. My shoes grew soggy with dew.

Finally, in the field, I reached her and walked in silence by her side.

Pink light was making a bubble on the edge of the hill. It spread out, slowly, like jam. Bumblebees clinging to flower petals were still cold and asleep and unaware.

"Look. Fairies' washing!" whispered Nanna.

Fairies? Maybe Dad was right about Nanna's imagination. But then I saw what Nanna meant: glistening, like strings of pearls. Like lace, the fairies' washing hung from fences, flowers, grass. It was exactly what a fairy would wear.

"Every morning the fairies hang their washing out to dry. But soon after sunup, it's gone." Nanna smiled and said it just like truth. But I knew I'd have to see that for myself.

Nanna marched off, as if she had a goal. It was the big rock by the lake. To my surprise, she climbed it, then stood atop, like a queen.

She was looking at something. But what? I couldn't tell.

Finally I saw pale gray forms: great blue herons. There were more than I had ever seen.

"Soon they'll spread out, around the countryside," said Nanna.

A few took off, with slow, wide wingbeats. More followed, and circled the lake. They dropped their shadows near our feet, then disappeared beyond the trees.

"The jewel birds?" I asked. Nanna didn't answer. Her eyes were closed. Her wrinkles stood out. The sun made her face glow a strange kind of gold.

"What are you doing, Nanna?"

"I'm being thankful," she replied. Then she scrambled down the rock and smiled. Thankful seemed a good way to be. We walked farther, near some trees.

"Nanna . . ."

"Shh!" She made the silence sign.

She mouthed the words: "the jewel bird." We crept toward a small tree. She pointed something out.

It didn't look like a jewel to me. It was only a tiny bird. Nanna pulled aside a branch. The sun shone on the bird. It was greenish, and still. And dead.

Or so I thought. I soon saw I was wrong. The bird flapped its wings and rose into the air.

As it turned toward the sun, its throat flashed ruby red.

It was a jewel bird! Now I could see. My breath

caught inside my chest. The bird flew past me, so close its wings made a breeze in my hair.

"A ruby-throated hummingbird," Nanna said. Now I knew why Nanna got up so early: for this . . . and more. She showed me other morning sights—meadowlarks singing, their golden feathers puffed.

A family of turkeys fed by the woods—I sneezed and they ran.

A mother deer and her fawn drank from a stream. We held our breath and stood still and watched.

But then the sun rose higher, baking hot. As we started to leave the field, I turned for a last look at the fairies' washing. But it had all disappeared.

I ran and searched. It was nowhere to be found.

Spiderwebs hung where the washing had been.

We were sitting in the kitchen, drinking hot chocolate, by the time my folks, their eyes half-closed, walked in. Nanna and I exchanged a secret smile. We had already seen the world.

***

April Pulley Sayre *is the acclaimed author of fifty-one children's books, including* Lake and Pond *(Twenty-First Century, 1996) and* Secrets of Sound: Studying the Calls of Whales, Elephants, and Birds *(Houghton Mifflin, 2002). She is a* madrugadora, *which in Spanish means "early riser."*

Chicago Waters

SUSAN POWER

Cities such as Chicago, Milwaukee, and Gary sit right on the shores of Lake Michigan, giving residents of houses and high-rises daily access to an expansive, restless wilderness. As Susan Power writes in this essay, the wildness of Lake Michigan was a welcome, if humbling, force during her growing-up years on Chicago's south shore.

My mother used to say that by the time I was an old woman, Lake Michigan would be the size of a silver dollar. She pinched her index finger with her thumb to show me the pitiful dimensions.

"People will gather around the tiny lake, what's left of it, and cluck over a spoonful of water," she told me.

I learned to squint at the 1967 shoreline until I had carved away the structures and roads built on landfill, and could imagine the lake and its city as my mother found them in 1942 when she arrived in Chicago. I say *the lake and its city* rather than *the city and its lake* because my mother taught me another secret: the city of Chicago belongs to Lake Michigan.

When my mother watches the water from her lakeside apartment building, she still sucks in her breath. "You have to respect the power of that lake," she tells me. "You see, no matter how much the city fathers tried to tame that water, it goes wild whenever it wants to. So you respect this powerful being."

And I do now. I do.

I was fifteen years old when I learned that the lake did not love me or hate me, but could claim me, nevertheless. I was showing off for a boy, my best friend, Tommy, who lived in the same building. He usually accompanied me when I went for a swim, but on this particular day he decided the water was too choppy. I always preferred the lake when it was agitated because its temperature warmed, transforming it into a kind of jacuzzi.

Tommy is right, I thought, once I saw the looming swells that had looked so unimpressive from the twelfth floor. Waves crashed against the breakwater wall and the metal ladder that led into and out of the lake like the entrance to the deep end of a swimming pool.

I shouldn't do this, I told myself, but I noticed Tommy watching me from his first-floor window. "I'm not afraid," I said to him under my breath. "I bet you think that I'll chicken out just because I'm a girl."

It had been a hot summer of dares, some foolish, some benign. Sense was clearly wanting. I took a deep breath and leaped off the wall into the turmoil, since the ladder was under attack. How did I think I would get out of the water? I hadn't thought that far. I bobbed to the surface and was instantly slapped in the face. I was beaten by water, smashed under again and again, until I began choking because I couldn't catch my breath.

I'm going to die now, I realized, and my heart filled with sorrow for my mother, who had already lost a husband and would now lose a daughter. I fought the waves, struggled to reach the air and the light, the sound of breakers swelling in my ears, unnaturally loud, like the noise of judgment day. *Here we go,* I thought.

Then I surprised myself, becoming unusually calm. I managed a quick gasp of breath and plunged to the bottom of the lake, where the water was a little quieter. I swam to the beach next door, remaining on the lake floor until I reached shallow waters. I burst to the surface then, my lungs burning, and it took me nearly five minutes to walk fifteen feet, knocked off balance as I was by waves that sucked at my legs. This beach now belongs to my mother and the other shareholders in her building, property recently purchased and attached to their existing lot. But in 1977 it was owned by someone else, and a barbed-wire fence separated the properties. I ended my misadventure by managing to climb over the sharp wire.

I remained downstairs until I stopped shaking. Tommy no longer watched me from his window, bored by my private games, unaware of the danger. I didn't tell my mother what had happened until hours later. I was angry at myself for being so foolish, so careless with my life, but I was never for a moment angry at the lake. I didn't come to fear it either, though it is a mighty force that drops 923 feet in its deepest heart. I understood that it struck indifferently; I was neither target nor friend. My life was my own affair, to lose or to save. Once I stopped struggling with the great lake, I flowed through it, and was expelled from its hectic mouth.

My mother still calls Fort Yates, North Dakota, *home,* despite the fact that she has lived in Chicago for nearly fifty-five years. She has taken me to visit the Standing Rock Sioux

Reservation, where she was raised, and although a good portion of it was flooded during the construction of the Oahe Dam, she can point to hills and buttes and creeks of significance. If I try to see the world through my mother's eyes, find the point where my own flesh falls to earth, I realize my home is Lake Michigan, the source of so many lessons.

As a teenager I loved to swim in the dark, to dive beneath the surface where the water was as black as the sky. The lake seemed limitless and so was I, an arm, a leg, a wrist, a face indistinguishable from the wooden boards of a sunken dock, from the sand I squeezed between my toes. I always left reluctantly, loath to become a body again and to feel more acutely the oppressive pull of gravity.

My father was the one who taught me to swim, with his usual patience and clear instructions. First he helped me float, his hands beneath my back and legs, his torso shading me from the sun. Next he taught me to flutter-kick, and I tried to make as much noise as possible. I dog-paddled in circles as a little girl, but my father swam in a straight line perpendicular to shore, as if he were trying to leave this land forever. Just as he had left New York state after a lifetime spent within its borders, easily—without regret. His swim was always the longest, the farthest. Mom and I would watch him as we lounged on our beach towels, nervous that a boat might clip him. It was a great relief to see him turn around and coast in our direction.

"Here he comes," Mom would breathe. "He's coming back now."

My father also showed me how to skip a stone across the water. He was skillful, and could make a flat rock bounce like a tiny, leaping frog, sometimes five or six hops before it sank to the bottom. It was the only time I could imagine this distinguished, silver-haired gentleman as a boy, and I laughed at him affectionately because the difference in our years collapsed.

I have gone swimming in other places—a chlorinated pool in Hollywood, the warm waters of the Caribbean, the Heart River in North Dakota—only to be disappointed and emerge unrefreshed. I am too used to Lake Michigan and its eccentricities. I must have cold, fresh water. I must have the stinking corpses of silver alewives floating on the surface as an occasional nasty surprise, discovered dead and never alive. I must have sailboats on the horizon and steel mills on the southern shore, golf balls I can find clustered around submerged pilings (shot from the local course), and breakwater boulders heavy as tombs lining the shore. I must have sullen lifeguards who whistle at anyone bold enough to stand in three feet of water, and periodic arguments between wind and water, which produce tearing waves and lake-spattered windows.

When I was little, maybe seven or eight, my parents and I went swimming in a storm. The weather was mild when we first set out, but the squall arrived quickly, without warning, as often happens in the Midwest. I remember we swam anyway, keeping an eye on the lightning not yet arrived from the north. There was no one to stop us, since we were dipping into deep water between beaches, in an area that was unpatrolled. The water was warmer than usual, the same temperature as the air, and when the rain wet the sky I leaped up and down in the growing waves, unable to feel the difference between air and water, lake and rain. The three of us played together that time, even my father remained near shore rather than striking east to swim past the white buoys. We were joined in this favorite element, splashing, ducking. I waved my arms over my head. My father pretended to be a great whale, heavy in the surf, now and then spouting streams of water from his mouth. He chased me. My mother laughed.

Dad died in 1973, when I was eleven years old, before my mother and I moved to the apartment on the lake. We always thought it such a shame he didn't get to make that move with us. He would so have enjoyed finding Lake Michigan in his backyard.

We buried him in Albany, New York, because that is where he was raised. My mother was born in North Dakota, and I was born between them, in Chicago. There is a good chance we shall not all rest together, our stories playing out in different lands. But I imagine that if a rendezvous is possible, and my mother insists it is, we will find one another in this great lake, this small sea that rocks like a cradle.

Raised in Chicago, **Susan Power** *received her undergraduate and law degrees from Harvard before deciding to become a full-time writer. Among her first published works are* The Grass Dancer, *a novel, and* Roofwalker, *a collection of stories and essays.*

Miracle

GWEN HART

We dreamt
of ice skating,
worn out,
whispering,
on the flinty bank
of the river.
We couldn't afford
skates, but carved
imaginary eights
with our boot-soles,
balled fists
punched together
for warmth.
Your breath
circled up
like a halo,
cloudy and brief.
The moon
made the snow
on our jackets
glisten
like sequins,
and we floated,

we glided
over the water
in our heavy,
brown shoes.

Gwen Hart *grew up in Painesville, Ohio, near Lake Erie. She holds degrees from Wellesley College and Hollins University. Several of her poems appear in the anthology* I Have My Own Song for It: Modern Poems about Ohio, *edited by William Greenway and Elton Glaser.*

Moon Magic

SIGURD F. OLSON

A full moon is not just a magnificent presence in the night sky; it's also a powerful force that tugs oceans to their highest tides and, some say, tugs on the wild and playful energies inside us all.

When the moon shines as it did last night, I am filled with unrest and the urge to range valleys and climb mountains. I want vistas of moonlit country from high places, must see the silver of roaring rapids and sparkling lakes. At such times I must escape houses and towns and all that is confining, be a part of the moon-drenched landscape and its continental sweep. It is only when the moon is full that I feel this way, only when it rises as it did last night, round and mellow as a great orange cheese over the horizon, slow-moving and majestic.

A quarter moon or a half or even a three-quarter moon does not do this to me, but when it is full my calm is gone and common things seem meaningless. All life is changed when the moon is full. Dogs howl madly when it comes into view and wolves make the hills resound with their wild music. Fish feed and throw themselves out of the water in sheer exuberance. Birds take to the air and sing in the glory of its light. Larger forms of game embark on galloping expeditions over their range. Under the full moon life is all adventure. . . .

So, when the moon shines as it did last night, I am apt to forget my work and responsibilities and take to the open, ranging the hills beneath its magic spell, tiring myself to the point where I can lie down and sleep in the full blaze of it. For me, this is the normal thing to do, and long ago I stopped trying to curb the impulse. I am merely being true to one of the most powerful influences within me, the reaction of protoplasm to lunar force.

If humans in all their sophistication permit moonlight to affect them, how much more does it affect animals? In my own moonlit wanderings I have had abundant occasion to see what it does and how animals in the wild respond to its charm. I have listened to loons go into ecstasies on wilderness lakes, have heard them call the whole night through and dash across the water as though possessed. I have heard sleepy birds begin to sing at midnight; wolves, foxes, frogs, and owls respond to the same inherent urge.

But the most delightful expression I know is the dance of the snowshoe hare in midwinter. If when the moon is bright you station yourself near a good rabbit swamp and stay quiet, you may see it, but you will need patience and endurance, for the night must be cold and still. Soon they begin to emerge, ghostly shadows with no spot of color except the black of their eyes. Down the converging trails they come, running and chasing one another up and down the runways, cavorting crazily in the light.

If you are weary and have seen enough, make a swoosh like the sound of wings and instantly each rabbit will freeze in its tracks, waiting for death to strike. But they are not still for long. As soon as the danger is past, they begin their game again. Very seldom do they leave the safety of their runways

and the protecting woods, but once last winter I found the lone track of a snowshoe rabbit several hundred yards from cover and knew that the moon had got the best of him and that under its spell he had left the woods and struck out boldly across the open field. To make sure that nothing had happened, I followed his track, expecting at any moment to see that foolish trail end with a couple of broad wingtips marking it on either side, or in a bloody snarl of fur where a dog or a prowling fox had come upon him. But the tracks went on and on, circling grandly the drifts and stone piles of the meadow. At last they headed back to the woods, but the final jumps were wide and desperate and I knew that the moon magic had worn thin. That rabbit, I concluded, must have been very young and foolish or very old and sure.

Once when camped on a rocky point along the Canadian border with the moon at full and my tent pitched in the light of it, I was lying in my sleeping bag, tent flaps open, studying the effect of pine needles etched against the sky. Suddenly I was aware of a slight rustle as though some small animal was trying to climb the silken roof of the tent. Then I saw that it was a mouse scrambling desperately up the edge of the side wall. For a moment it hesitated, then slipped backward, and I thought it surely must fall. Another wild scramble and it was on the ridge rope itself, tottering uncertainly back and forth. Then, to my amazement, the mouse launched itself out into space and slid down the smooth and shining surface of the tent to the ground below.

The action was repeated many times until the little animal became expert and reckless and lost no time between the climb back and the sheer abandon of its slide. Faster and faster it ran, intoxicated now by its new and thrilling experience; up along the edge straight toward the center of the ridge rope, a swift leap, belly down, legs spread wide to get the full effect of the exhilarating toboggan it had found, a slide of balloon silk straight to the needle-strewn ground below.

I watched the game for a long time. Eventually I stopped trying to count the slides and wondered at last how the mouse could possibly keep up its pace. As I lay there, I became convinced that it was enjoying itself hugely, that I was witnessing an activity which had no purpose but pleasure. I had seen many animals play in the moonlight—had watched a family of otters enjoying a slide into a deep pool, beaver playing a game of tag in a pond, squirrels chasing one another wildly through the silver-splashed tops of the pines. Under the magic spell of the moon, the mouse had acted no differently than the rest.

I thought as I lay there in my bag that, if nothing else, moonlight made animals and men forget for a little while the seriousness of living; that there were moments when life could be good and play the natural outlet for energy. I knew that if man could abandon himself as my deer mouse had done and slide down the face of the earth in the moonlight once a month—or once a year, perhaps—it would be good for his soul.

Sigurd F. Olson *spent his adult life in the Boundary Waters region of northern Minnesota and the adjoining Quetico Provincial Park in southwestern Ontario. He was the author of many books about this region, including* The Singing Wilderness, *from which this excerpt is taken.*

A Clutch of Flowers

PHYLLIS I. HARRIS

Get out of town beyond the truckstop
    Where blooms collide at the side of the road.
Run through tall, unforgiving grass
Scale the ditch
Beat off bugs
Sneeze the dust
Snatch Queen Anne's lace,
    flirty-eyed Susans,
      milkweed's princely pompons,
        and lemon lily's macho cousin, Tiger.

Lordy, how they glorify and vie
    like streetkids—
    wild things
    taunting, teasing, pressing into the wind
And me.

Phyllis I. Harris *gathered wildflowers and grandchildren while teaching kindergarten and collecting a B.A. from the University of Minnesota, an M.Ed. from the University of Illinois, and an M.F.A. from Norwich University.*

The Ice Deer

ELLEN CREAGER

Almost everyone who has lived beside a lake in northern Great Lakes country has seen or heard about a deer getting trapped out on the ice. This story describes one such encounter on the frozen shores of Lake St. Clair.

The night we saw the deer on the lake, it was January.

We had gone to Pier Park to go sledding, but the snow was chippy and my saucer bumped so hard it jolted my back, and the wind was so freezing that even my eyeballs were cold. Then my little sister Caitlin's purple scarf blew away. We watched it skip over piles of snow into the parking lot. She wailed.

"I'll get it!" I shouted to Dad, who picked up my crying sister and watched me run.

The scarf snagged briefly on the antenna of a Jeep and blew there like a flag. I snatched it off and just as I did, my dad and Caitlin caught up with me.

"Mine!" my teary sister said, holding her four-year-old hand out for the scarf. Dad took it and wrapped it safely around her chubby neck.

"Thanks, Mandy. You're pretty fast for a twelve-year-old," Dad said, and I laughed because I was only eleven. "Let's go look at the lake before we go," Dad said.

We walked to the pier, then stood side by side at the wooden railing looking out onto the gloomy mist of Lake St. Clair.

It was not a deep lake. It was not a big lake. It was not a Great Lake. But it was my lake. If you look on a map, you'll see it. To the north, it connects to the St. Clair River, which goes straight up to Lake Huron. To the south, it connects to the big Detroit River, which goes down to Lake Erie. In the olden days, somebody forgot to include Lake St. Clair as one of the Great Lakes, so it has to be satisfied with just being a helper lake, kind of like Huron and Erie are the grown-up lakes and St. Clair is the kid lake, and the rivers are the hands that hold them all together.

In the winter, ice stops the freighters from running, so that night we saw none. If we looked really hard, we could see the shoreline of Canada, just a slash of black in the distance. Some of the lake was covered with ice, but out in the middle it was gray, rough water. I shivered and stood closer to Dad. Wind blew in our faces, and I could feel more snow on the way.

"Let's go," I said, tugging his hand. "I'm cold."

As we started to turn away from the lake, I saw the deer. Dad saw her too, out on the ice about six feet from the pier, standing still as a stone, her large brown eyes staring at us with silent fear.

"Doggie!" shouted Caitlin, pointing at the animal. "Doggie!"

"Hush," Dad said, creeping closer to the railing. "How'd that deer get out there, I wonder? Looks like she's stuck on the ice."

"Let's go get her," I said, and I slipped under the railing, my boots dangling over the side. I felt a hand grab my coat and jerk me upright.

"No, Mandy, the ice isn't safe," Dad warned. He hauled me roughly to my feet, and I realized Dad was scared, too. Scared for the deer, and scared for me.

"We'll have to call the police," Dad said. "Mandy, you stay here and watch the deer. And don't move!" he commanded. "I'll run to the guardhouse and get help." He hurried away through the dusk with Caitlin bouncing wildly in his arms.

I turned back to the ice. I looked at the deer. She looked at me. I looked at her. She looked at me. Her nose quivered. Her white tail flickered. Her long legs splayed out, sliding on the ice, and she scrambled to find her footing, but couldn't. Panicky, she stood still. She made no sound. The wind whipped across the ice, and darkness fell.

Footsteps. Running. Dad again. His face. I was so glad to see him.

"Dad, she can't move! She's scared!" I said, leaning into his ear. "We have to help her. She might die." I pointed at the frightened animal, who seemed to be farther away now. Maybe the ice was shifting. Or maybe she was becoming invisible in the gloom.

"They're coming," Dad said. "I left Caitlin in the guardhouse eating a candy bar, and I called Mom to come get her. Do you want to go home?"

"No!" I said. "I have to stay." Dad didn't try to talk me out of it. He just nodded.

"OK, we'll stay."

Minutes ticked by in the cold. The deer scrabbled with her feet, trying to get her balance, but she was in danger with every motion, and seemed to know it. The ice had long spidery cracks in it. I could hear it creak and moan in the night wind. A tiny thread of panic rose in my chest. What if she floated out to the open water? Could she swim? Would she freeze?

We saw flashing lights, and soon the Point Carey police cruiser arrived. Dad pointed to the deer on the ice. The officer said, "OK, we'll need the Coast Guard," and got on his radio.

One officer got a long stick with a loop at the end and tried to lean over the railing to hook the deer's neck. But he was too far away.

"Ice isn't safe," he shouted over his bulky shoulder as he gave up. I could have told him that. He talked too loud. Couldn't he see the deer was afraid?

Dad pushed me toward the warm police car and told me to wait inside until more help arrived. I tore my eyes away from the deer and climbed into the back of the car with its fuzzy seats. My fingertips tingled and my eyes watered and I tried not to cry like some scared little kid.

"It's going to be OK," I whispered to myself, digging my nails into my palms, the pain distracting me from my tears. "It's going to be OK."

Finally we saw a light from around the edge of the park, on the ice. We heard a motor. It was a red and white Coast Guard hovercraft, a little boat that can skim over ice and is used to save fishermen and other people trapped on the lake. But how could it save a deer?

Dad came over and opened the car door, and I scrambled out for a better look.

"Over here," shouted one of the police officers, waving his arms. The boat's big spotlight swung slowly toward the trapped deer, whose front legs were bent inward and starting to sag. As the boat drew quietly closer, she tried to back away, and the ice she stood on cracked more. A man stood in the boat with a gun. I screamed.

"Don't shoot her! Dad, they're shooting at her!" I ran toward the ice and started to slide under the railing again. I had to save her. They couldn't, couldn't kill her.

"Wait, Mandy!" Dad ran after me. "They're going to tranquilize her, that's all!" A police officer grabbed my arm and jerked me upward. "Get her out of the way," he said gruffly, and shoved me toward my father. Dad put his arms around me.

"You don't have to watch," he said, and I turned and buried my head in his wool jacket.

Crack. The rifle went off. I heard a thud. I heard the boat motor, and men talking. I peered up. The deer was on her side now, and she looked like she was dead. The men put a rope around her big body and dragged her onto a big blue tarp on the ice. Then the boat slowly chugged away around the point, pulling the tarp along. Dad grabbed my hand.

"Come on, let's see what happens next," he said, and we ran down the pier and across the sidewalk, past the pools and the sledding hill, around to the woods, and onto the beach where in the summer I swam and drank Slurpees, though that seemed incredible now.

The Coast Guard boat hovered just off shore, while men, now out of the boat and on the thin ice, grabbed the tarp with the deer and hauled it in. We ran to help. At the edge of the beach, I grabbed the side of the tarp.

Oh, she was heavy, and up close, she looked beautiful and still. I pulled one mitten off with my teeth and, so nobody could see, I touched the fur on her back. It was wiry, but soft. Her white tail and white ears shone in the garish spotlight. We heaved and dragged her up the bank.

"OK, leave her here," said one of the Coast Guard men. "She'll wake up soon." They left the deer lying on the blue tarp, safely off the ice, then piled into their boat and sped away, other rescues to make. The police officers waited with us.

Snow began falling—I knew that it would—and Dad and I huddled together, watching the deer by only a dim park light. Suddenly, her legs jerked. Her eyes drifted open. We backed away, behind some picnic tables. She lay there for a few minutes. Was she hurt? Sick?

Then she rolled. She climbed up on her unsteady legs, glanced around. Dry land. No more shifting underfoot. She stared at me for a moment, her velvety black eyes showing nothing but how it felt to be a deer, and scared, and alive.

A second more. She bolted and ran toward the woods.

She lived.

Tears streaming down my face, I watched her go and something in my heart ached with joy and sorrow. She was like the wind, and I wished I could run that fast. And I hoped she was safe in the woods and had a mother and father deer who would never, ever let her go on the ice again, and maybe they would yell at her for scaring them half to death and then take her home. I put my mittened hand in Dad's big glove.

"Let's go now," I said. I looked at Dad, and his eyes were tearing up, too.

"How about ice cream?" he asked. I nodded. We walked to the guardhouse. And there Caitlin and Mom, who had not gone home after all, were waiting for us.

Ellen Creager *is a Michigan native who has never lived more than a few miles from the Great Lakes. She now resides in southeastern Michigan with her husband and four teenage daughters. A reporter at the* Detroit Free Press, *she was nominated for the 2001 Pulitzer Prize in feature writing.*

The Gold Medal Flower

GENE STRATTON-PORTER

Collecting plants in northern Indiana may sound like a relatively tame activity. But for Gene Stratton-Porter, the quest for a new botanical find brought with it both thrills and danger. One year in the early 1900s, a publishing company offered a gold medal to the first person who could bring back from the wilds a live fringed gentian. Stratton-Porter was already searching for the flower, but the contest drove her to near obsession. In the process, she lived through one of the most frightening afternoons of her collecting career.

The quest started in late August. I had studied everything I could find concerning *Gentiana crinata*. I could have drawn diagrams of it that would have been perfectly accurate. So, also, could each of my three helpers. The search led us through every stretch of swamp country in a county that boasted three hundred lakes, over one hundred of which were large enough to be named and charted. I had no book that listed the flower before September, but earlier in the season, in a spot that looked propitious, I sighted a blue that tempted me. Somewhere beside the road my field automobile was standing; somewhere in the surrounding swamps my driver and my secretary were waiting for me, and just as I entered the swampy stretch I saw going down the road the lean, raw-boned figure of Eve, a six-foot Pennsylvania woman who was at that time my cook, a woman of British extraction who fairly worshipped a flower, a woman with such a sense of fineness and of inherent beauty in her nature that she grew incoherent when she was turned loose on these made roads of northern Indiana that led through acres of swamps where lakes touched borders in chains often of twenty-mile length, where every flower and bird that ever sought such a location was in evidence.

Eve was galloping down the road with her head up, her nostrils distended, the last I saw of her. I was making my way from hummock to hummock over ground that quivered under my feet, lured several rods in the distance by a hint of blue half concealed by tufted marsh grasses. I was so intent on my objective that I was in to my knees before I fully realized that I was sinking, and then there ran through me with a sickening throb a feeling that I once before had experienced in a swamp in southern Michigan, a parting of things to let me down, a closing in on the feet, a pull as if a giant throat had begun to swallow me and never meant to let me go. The first thought that came to me was that I must not remain in an up-standing position, so I threw myself full length toward the stoutest looking hummock I could see, spread my arms as widely as I could, and sought with each hand for something to which I could cling. I have no idea how much time elapsed before I worked one foot loose and brought it to the surface. Then I drew it up to my side as a frog draws up its hind leg, and with all my might I worked to swing the other foot where the one I had released had been, and finally I succeeded in drawing it to the surface. I shall never forget the quivering throb under me when I planted my knees and tried to throw my body forward. . . . When I found that I was making slight if any headway, I remembered Eve; so with all my might I screamed for her, and presently I saw her coming.

Eve knew what quicksands meant. Only a few days before, in an effort to help me uproot an arrowhead lily, she had gone into uncertain footing herself and had started to sink, but a field man was with me and the two of us had been able to draw her out. I had only to shout: "Quicksands!" to bring her at a flying run. She was a much larger woman than I and heavier. I had to warn her back. I told her to make a raid on the rail fence that surrounded the swamp and as quickly as possible to bring a couple of rails. She was a strong woman and she brought two weather-beaten rails from the top of an old snake fence her first trip. Then I instructed her to take them one at a time, to come as near as she dared, to swing them lengthwise three or four times to gain propulsion, and then to throw them toward me. The first one landed a few inches out of my grasp, but by frantic work I reached it. The second one, guided by the experience gained in throwing the first, came truer. While Eve went for more rails, I managed, by as difficult work as I ever encountered in a lifetime of field work, to pull myself between and on the rails. Spreading my weight over as much surface as possible helped to keep me up, and by the time I had reached the end of the first rails Eve was ready with more, and when I came to the end of them I could take her hand, so by and by I lay nauseated, muck covered, and thankful on earth firm enough to bear my weight without danger.

As I describe this experience, I can see Eve getting down on her knees on the last rails she threw into the swamp and working her way out until she could reach the ends of the first ones she had thrown in, and then, one at a time, dragging them toward her. She might have been fairly sure that a foundation that would hold me would bear her weight, but she did take a risk and a nasty one in order that she might be able to return to the fence of an unknown farmer four rails that she had taken from it in an effort to help me to save my life. When I see the carelessness that people exhibit today in the handling of other people's property, the small regard that is paid to personal rights, there always rises to my mind the figure of this lean, gaunt Pennsylvania woman down on her knees struggling to rescue four rails at the very edge of one of the quicksands that dot the northern part of my state, many of them the surface outlets of subterranean passages the depth of which Indiana has no sounding line long enough to measure.

⌁

Gene Stratton-Porter *was born and raised in Indiana. From an early age, she devoted herself to the study and care of plants, moths, birds, and other living things. Besides documenting the lives of animals with her research and photography, she wrote several books of fiction and nonfiction, including* Girl of the Limberlost *and* Tales You Won't Believe, *from which this excerpt is drawn.*

From the Cellar

WILLIAM PITT ROOT

The sky came down in whirling cloud
that sucked up light and air
and found us trembling and glued
hand to hand by fear.

Eerie darkness, gloomy, green,
engulfed the world we knew—
we peered as from a submarine
through an abyssal maw.

But fear could not deflect the force
roaring crazed around us,
a train on its nightmare course
plunging through the house.

After, when we crept outside,
we stared, as from a dream—
The house was gone but one wall stood,
one door in its frame,

while down the road, miles away,
the twister, darkly dangling,
hung from the clearing summer sky,
hopped like a toy spring.

William Pitt Root *is a prize-winning poet who for many years commuted weekly between his work as a professor in New York City and his home in Arizona, where he was Poet Laureate of Tucson from 1997 to 2002. Recently, reluctantly, he shortened his commute by moving to North Carolina. He started writing in response to a seventh grade English teacher's assignment to write about something he'd seen to someone who had never seen it. "I chose to write about first seeing snow. I'd grown up in Florida but moved abruptly with my mother to Minnesota after my father was killed in an accident. I wrote about snow for my friends, but since I didn't know their addresses, I never sent the letters. Much of what I write still feels as if it's for a friend with whom I've somehow lost touch."*

Adrift on Niagara

CHARLES E. MISNER

Few places in the Great Lakes region have been the site of as much drama and danger as Niagara Falls—the spectacular waterfalls that plummet down the Niagara River between Lake Erie and Lake Ontario. In this essay, Charles Misner recounts a terrifying ordeal on the ice bridge that formed just above the falls in the winter of 1899. Ice bridges are caused by a particular set of weather events. A spell of warm winter weather that year broke up the ice on Lake Erie, sending ice chunks down the river, where they fractured and jammed. Then, when temperatures dropped again, the resulting ice jam solidified into a rough bridge. Locals and tourists alike enjoyed crossing the ice bridge. But deep crevices and high hummocks made travel perilous, and, as Misner and his friend discovered, an ice bridge can be far from stable.

On Sunday, January 22, 1899, my friend, Miss Bessie Hall, and I decided to visit Niagara Falls and cross, if possible, over the ice bridge. We found perhaps fifteen persons on the ice. I was very anxious to cross, but here Miss Hall faltered. After a little persuasion she agreed to follow. So we started; little did we know how we should return.

The ice at this point, towering as high as thirty and forty feet, was very rough; then again we would come to patches probably fifty feet long where the ice would range from the size of a teacup to pieces twenty-five feet in diameter. There was no path cut in the ice as the bridge had formed only a day or two before. Over this jagged ice we picked our way to perhaps two hundred yards from the boat landing. Here we sat down on a large boulder of ice. It was a grand scene and we sat there nearly half an hour. By this time many of the others had returned to shore and we found we were left alone. I felt perfectly safe, but Miss Hall remarked she could hear a singing noise under her feet. I assured her it was only her fancy.

Feeling we had seen all that could be seen we started back toward the American shore. We had not gone far when we were told by gestures that a landing at the boat dock was impossible, as the ice had broken away, leaving a crevice that was too large to cross. We were told to go down farther toward the arch bridge, where we could land in safety. I was not a bit afraid yet, but felt that when I was safe on land I would be thankful. I said nothing to Miss Hall, as she was naturally already a little alarmed. The traveling was very difficult as the ice was very rough. There were a good many people along the banks and on the bridge watching us, as we seemed, and were, in rather a dangerous position. By this time I began to be pretty well alarmed myself. Every minute or two we could hear a noise as if something were falling. We were now perhaps seventy-five yards from the steel arch bridge and about fifty feet from the American shore. Ranging along close to the American shore was a huge boulder of ice upon which were about seven or eight men.

So it was when the terrible crash came. We were hurrying as fast as possible and had just come to a large crevice in the ice about three feet across, which I tried to bridge over with pieces of ice so as to be able to help Miss Hall across. By looking into this crevice you could see the black water a hundred feet below. One false step meant sure death. It was now about 4:10 P.M. There had been probably two hundred people watching our progress and in less than three minutes afterwards there were two thousand.

I was just getting ready to jump across this crevice when there was a loud report, a grinding sound, and we realized that the ice bridge had begun to move. The falling of huge masses of ice, the grinding, gurgling sound that reached our ears nearly paralyzed us with fear. I was undecided at first as to the best course to take, but on finding ourselves entirely cut off from the American shore, our only escape was to head toward the Canadian side. Taking Miss Hall by the hand I started to make for a place of safety. We had perhaps gone a yard or so when the ice parted at our very feet and but for my having hold of Miss Hall's hand she would have gone to the bottom or have been ground to death by the ice before reaching the water. She fell her full length between these two boulders, but by putting forth every bit of strength I could I managed to pull her out, but none too soon, for the ice came together with an awful crash.

We were now about seventy-five or one hundred yards below the steel arch bridge, having been carried about one hundred and fifty or two hundred yards on the ice. Close to the steel bridge on the American side is the tunnel through which the water used in the power station above the Falls emerges at the rate of eighty-five miles an hour. Here was the point where death seemed so certain. Old settlers of Niagara Falls little expected us to get by this point, as the undercurrent here usually sucks under anything that passes. But we passed this in safety and, when a few yards below, we heard a shout and found that the ice bridge had come to a standstill! It was the first time in the memory of man that the bridge was ever known to stop after once starting down the river!

Now we realized we had to act and act quickly. Every second meant life or death. Shouts went up from the thousands on shore for us to hurry. The bridge was liable to start again at any moment. We headed straight for the Canadian bank. Men shouted to keep down the river farther. Taking Miss Hall by the arm, I made haste to reach land. Falling down but quickly jumping up we would again push onward. Once Miss Hall gave up entirely, but I succeeded in urging her onward. It was very difficult for us to run over this expanse of ice (about two hundred or three hundred yards across) and mostly huge boulders thirty feet high. Again it would be necessary for us to jump five and ten feet into ravines, not knowing where we were going. The ice was liable to break up at any moment. From our position we could see the thousands who were watching us and could hear the encouraging shouts as we neared the Canadian shore. It was necessary for me to leave Miss Hall at times in order to determine our best course.

After crossing about fifty yards of the slush ice we reached the Canadian shore, after being about forty-five minutes on the ice bridge struggling for our lives. There willing hands stood waiting to receive us and to congratulate us on our almost miraculous escape from certain death.

Charles E. Misner was a young traveling salesman from Buffalo when he traveled to Niagara in the winter of 1899. He wrote about his adventures on the ice bridge in the March 1899 issue of Home *magazine.*

Return Portage

LOUIS JENKINS

First the canoe,
400 rods over a hilly trail,
then back for the packs
and the fishing poles
and one last look at the lake.

I wish it would always be like this.
Move up, go back,
pick everything up,
leave nothing
but the pines,
the lake,
the fall afternoon.

Louis Jenkins *lives in Duluth, Minnesota. He is the author of several books of poetry, the most recent of which is* The Winter Road *(Holy Cow! Press, 2000).*

Winter Season

BRUCE CATTON

In a typical winter, the northern parts of Michigan receive more than a hundred and fifty inches of snow, and lakes and rivers freeze over for months at a time. In this excerpt from his memoir, Bruce Catton explains how deep snow and slick ice form the basis for all great winter adventures.

In some ways winter was the most exciting season of all, especially during the first few weeks. After that it began to seem endless, and by the middle of February we began to feel as if we had been frozen in forever, but at first it was fun. We did not do as much skating as might be supposed, because the unbroken ice on Crystal Lake usually was covered with a foot or two of snow, but we could sometimes clear the surface of a convenient millpond, and a January thaw followed by a hard freeze might make the lake serviceable. A couple of miles to the east of us an electric light company had dammed the Betsie River to provide current for the surrounding villages, and the flooded valley above the dam often provided good skating. That was an eerie place to go. Trees killed by the rising waters stuck their dead tips through the ice, and to skate there just at dusk was like skating through a haunted forest. Once we got around the bend from the dam we might have been a thousand miles from anywhere, with nothing in sight but the ghostly gray dead trees, and no sound except for the ring of skates on ice. It was a little frightening, especially so because there were air holes around some of the trees, although I do not remember that anybody ever came to grief there; anyway, it was good to be on the way back to town again, with skates slung over the shoulder and the mind full of the warmth and the good supper that would be waiting when we got home.

We did a good deal of skiing, in a makeshift sort of way. All of the skis were homemade—a local carpenter would produce a pair for a modest sum—and they lacked modern refinements; there was simply a leather strap on each ski to put your toe through, with nothing to go around your heel and bind you firmly to the skis. Maneuvers that are taken for granted by present-day skiers were utterly beyond our reach, but we could go swinging down the open slopes at a great rate, and glide across country in fine style, and since we did not know that we lacked anything we were completely satisfied. It did not enter our heads that we ought to wear special costumes, or that to go skiing was to indulge in a sophisticated, socially rewarding activity. We did it because it was fun.

The best sport of all in the winter was coasting downhill. Go where you chose, from the center of the village, and you soon came to a road that went down a long hill. The one to the west went down such an easy slope that it did not offer much; and the one to the north was too dangerous, because it was steep and it led straight into the main street of Beulah, where some farmer was apt to be pulling away from the curb to make a U-turn with a two-horse team and a heavy wagon-box on runners just as a bobsled full of youngsters, moving at better than thirty miles an hour and all but out of control, came barreling

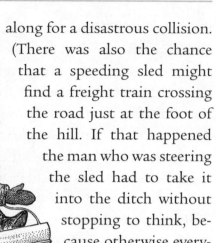

along for a disastrous collision. (There was also the chance that a speeding sled might find a freight train crossing the road just at the foot of the hill. If that happened the man who was steering the sled had to take it into the ditch without stopping to think, because otherwise everybody would get killed.) In the end the village council made coasting on Beulah hill illegal, and the rule was pretty generally observed.

The east hill road was equally steep but less dangerous because there was no town at the foot of it. There was a railroad crossing there, to be sure, but the Ann Arbor railroad did not run many trains and we had a fair idea of the schedules, and there were massive drifts along both sides of the highway in case one had to bail out in a hurry. When a bobsled ran into one of these drifts at high speed there was always a hilarious mix-up; the sled would come to a most abrupt stop and the five or six occupants would be catapulted off into the snow, landing head downward as likely as not. One time Robert and I took our mother down this hill, because she had never gone coasting and wanted to see what it was like. Just as we went down the steepest part, whirling along at a prodigious clip, she concluded that it was like nothing she wanted any more of and she firmly ordered: "Robert! Robert, *stop* it!" We were dutiful sons and always did what our parents told us to do, so

Robert obediently guided the sled into a deep drift. As anyone but Mother would have known, the sled stopped but its passengers did not. Mother, who was no lightweight, shot through the air like a rocketing partridge, going completely over Robert's head and coming down wrong-end up in five feet of powdery snow. It took us several minutes to get her out, because she was laughing so hard that she was unable to act in her own behalf. I do not recall that she ever went coasting again.

The best coasting was down the long road that went to the south. Here the slope was more gentle, but when the snow was packed right you could move fairly fast, and you could go on almost forever; with luck, a bobsled could reach the Betsie River bridge, a full mile from the starting point. That meant a long walk back, but nobody seemed to mind. Going down the long slope was effortless and silent, and since we were not more than eight inches off the ground the speed seemed much faster than it really was. A ride like that was worth a long walk.

I remember once some of us went down that hill after dark. We went all the way to the bridge, and as the sled slowed down to a halt we sat motionless as long as there was the least chance of gliding forward another foot. We gave up, finally, turned the sled around, and started pulling it back up hill. It was cold, and a north wind was whipping dry snow off of the surrounding fields with a soft, rustling noise. The wind seemed to come straight down from the north pole—really, there was nothing between us and the pole to stop it—and it came out of the emptiness of the everlasting ice, as if the old darkness once again was sliding down from the top of the world to swallow everything; perhaps that was what made the ghostly creeping little sound out across the snowdrifts. I shivered, not because I wanted a warmer coat but because I wanted some sort of reassurance, which did not seem to be forthcoming. Yet overhead all the stars were out, and on the frozen road I could hear the sound of laughter.

Bruce Catton *recorded his memories of his boyhood years in Michigan in his memoir,* Waiting for the Morning Train, *from which this excerpt is drawn. Among his other publications are more than a dozen books on U.S. history.*

Great Places

Fireworks!

KATHARINE CRAWFORD ROBEY

Michigan's western coast is lined with sand dunes that rise as high as four hundred feet above Lake Michigan's waters. From here, one can watch sunsets, shooting stars, and other brilliant celestial displays.

Julia pushed her bare feet through the cold sand, plowing a quick furrow. The sand on the beach felt like silk, cold silk, tonight. In all of her ten summers, she could not remember a Fourth of July in northwest Michigan this cold. She sat down to slip her sneakers back on and surveyed the bundled-up crowd of resorters and townspeople, looking for her dad. As soon as they'd left the car, her older sister, Marilyn, had taken him by the hand and propelled him away from her. Now, disappointed, she saw not Dad, but Marilyn, running back toward her.

"Ju-li-a!" Marilyn said, stopping. "What are you doing down there?" Marilyn towered above her like the lighthouse at the end of the breakwater. "Come on! The fireworks are about to start."

"Wait!" Julia said, her attention drawn to the evening sky above town. "Look up at the stars! They look like sparklers, they're so clear."

"Will you forget the stars for once," Marilyn said impatiently. "I'm going. Dad's in our regular spot. You can find us."

By the time Julia looked away from the sky, Marilyn had disappeared. Now Julia, too, hurried toward the small bluff where Dad would be sitting. Chilled, she pressed through families huddled together on the sand, blankets pulled around them.

She glanced across the smooth water to the horizon. The sun was down. A rosy tint lay across the great lake and over the lumpy crowd on the shore. Undaunted by the cold, yachts floated as usual in the harbor, their masts decorated with twinkling white lights. She could hear the tooting of their horns, punctuated by the blast of firecrackers set off near the water's edge. She stopped for a second. Perhaps it was the cold that made everything look so beautiful.

"Over here!" Marilyn signaled from their blanket. Julia glimpsed Dad at the far end of the blanket, not in the middle as she'd hoped. Her older sister had taken the spot next to him! Shivering, she sat next to Marilyn and pulled the end of the blanket over her bare legs. Dad couldn't get up to the cottage much in the summertime, and he was leaving again in the morning. Julia kicked at the sand.

She could hear snatches of their conversation. They were talking about the drive-in movies they'd seen last night at the Cherry Bowl. Julia, down with a sore throat, hadn't gone. All day Marilyn had boasted about staying out with Dad till one in the morning.

The crowd was stirring, restless for the fireworks to begin. "Why don't they start? It's dark enough. It's ten o'clock."

Marilyn seemed unaware of anything but Dad. She was still talking to him about the second movie they'd seen, something about a man and a woman getting locked in an Egyptian tomb.

Julia looked behind them at the stars. They were even brighter now and more beautiful. He'd want to see them, wouldn't he? She leaned over Marilyn, determined to interrupt.

But a resounding boom startled her before she could speak. She put her hands over her ears. The fireworks had started. She was too late.

"Should have brought earplugs," Marilyn said, leaning back against the sand, yawning.

Umbrellas of colored lights burst above their heads, then fell into the still, black water. The crowd oohed and aahed and applauded. There were more colors this summer than Julia had ever seen before. Some fell into the lake in tinseled streams of red, green, and blue. But her favorites were the glittering fountains of pure white light that reminded her of the stars themselves.

After each shower of color, she could see Dad lean over to Marilyn and hear him say, "That was the best," or "The green lights are new this year," or "This is great!" Then Marilyn would giggle and nod. Marilyn was always giggling and nodding.

Then the bursts and booms became farther apart. During each pause, the crowd murmured, "Is that all?" Voices drifted to her across the sand, saying, "Last year there was a grand finale," and "It gets shorter every year." Then there would be another boom and burst of light, and the crowd would quiet down. Finally, not too soon for the cold ones, there came one last prolonged burst of every color, as if in that last burst of artificial light there lay a secret. But Julia knew it wasn't so.

The cold north air hurried them back to their car. As usual, Marilyn rushed for the front door. But this time, Dad opened the back door and gestured at Marilyn. "Why don't you let Julia sit up front with me?" Julia saw Marilyn screw up her face and sit down, slouching, in back. As they drove out Michigan Avenue, Julia could hear Marilyn behind her, yawning loudly.

Then they turned off onto Sutter Road. Marilyn had stopped yawning and was perfectly quiet—for once. Say something, Julia told herself. You have Dad all alone. For once in your life tell him something that means something to you. Something grown-up.

They reached the tunnel of trees that she loved so much and then the meadow that she loved even more. The meadow where twice she'd seen a red fox trot across the road during the day, when she'd been with Mom. Tell him that, she thought. But she was quiet.

Soon they'd be home. She stole a glance at the backseat. Marilyn had her eyes closed, and her head was bobbing against her chest. She was asleep! Now was the time to say something.

Suddenly, Julia saw a light streak across the top of the sky. "Dad? Did you see that?" It came again. They were almost across the bridge over the Platte River, by the campgrounds.

"See what?" he said.

"The light. In the sky. Turn, Dad, turn! Turn and go to the mouth of the Platte! It's happening again! Don't you see it?"

They were almost past the turnoff. He peered above the steering wheel and then, suddenly, turned left, tires squealing. He sped toward the mouth. Julia could see more streaks now, but most of the sky was hidden by the trees. Dad drove fast. Julia worried he might hit a deer, but there were no deer crossing the road tonight.

Then Dad whirled into the gravel parking area and stopped the car on the crest that overlooks the Platte and Lake Michigan beyond. They jumped out of the car. Julia glanced at the backseat. Marilyn was still fast asleep. She hadn't even opened her eyes. As Julia turned away and took her dad's hand, she heard Marilyn stir and say, "Are we home yet?" Neither of them answered. The northern lights were all around them.

They ran to the highest point. Out of the black night, streaks of white and green-white light spanned the sky in arch after arch. The whole sky was shimmering.

She felt her dad put his arm around her shoulder. "Aurora borealis," he said. "Nature's fireworks. I've never seen them like this. Never. If you hadn't been looking up, I'd have driven home and missed the whole thing."

The light was all around them. It was ghostly almost, in its awesome shining. She felt as if it might envelop her and Dad at any minute, even though she knew it wouldn't. He squeezed her shoulder. Then he said out loud what she was thinking, and she knew, for the first time, that he understood how she felt.

"Incredible," he said. "Far better than the fireworks at Frankfort."

Then, suddenly, she felt different. Big and little at the same time. Big, standing there next to her father on the dark bluff, just him and her. Little, compared to the streaks of shimmering light shooting through the heavens, surrounding them both.

"Dad? Marilyn's asleep."

"I know."

"She should see this."

He paused. Then he said quietly, as if the display were for them alone, but they should share it, "Go and wake Marilyn."

Every summer when **Katharine Crawford Robey** *was a child, her family would take the Lake Michigan car ferry from their winter home in Wisconsin to their summer cabin in Michigan. On the Fourth of July, they always watched the fireworks at the Frankfort beach. After the fireworks on one incredible night, they saw the northern lights at the mouth of the Platte, just like the girl in this story.*

Milwaukee River Poem

JULIE PARSON-NESBITT

I give back
to the weeds of Milwaukee
to a solitary morning of church bells
and a bristling skyline of sirens
arched against the blue Wisconsin night

I give back
to that afternoon when the street was silent
with maple trees burning in spiky air
and bumblebees drunk in the marigolds
sweet and rotten past their season

to that season of late summer light
of Milwaukee weeds, or wildflowers:
sky-blue chicory
boneset flowering by factory lots
where bindweed leapfrogs the iron-link fence
and goldenrod and late purple asters
parade among broken-necked bottles

I release
the midnights nauseous with desperation
into the slap and song of the girls jumping rope

and as for the dizzying days of secrets
I slip them under the rumble of car radios
when the teenage boys drive by

river and weed and streetsong
I take as absolution
like the craving for mint in my mouth
for the grit of sugar between my teeth

I give back
I give back
and I offer
other entry into this world:

the marshy margins of the river's recede
where old trees step out of the water
in an undertow of wind

or to any world, shining or dark,
dark or shining.

Julie Parson-Nesbitt *has received the Gwendolyn Brooks Poetry Award and two Academy of American Poets awards. Her poetry collection is* Finders *(West End Press). A Chicago writer, she has worked as a poet-in-the-schools and as executive director of the Guild Complex, a literary organization.*

At Uglyfish Lake

ELLEN AIRGOOD

The wildest country in the Great Lakes region lies around its most northern lake—Superior. The area has been home to Chippewa Indians, French explorers, copper miners, foresters, and many other people who have drawn their physical and emotional sustenance from this rugged terrain.

Listen. Let me tell you what my life is made of. Snow and ice. Cedar and hemlock. Fire and smoke.

The quiet of the days is deep.

I live on a lake called Muskallonge, far north in Michigan.

I live in a one-room cabin, cedar-shaked and tin-roofed, small beneath tall white pines.

I live at the end of the road five months a year. The sign two miles west says, "Seasonal Road, Not Snowplowed by the Luce County Road Commission."

I live near the big lake, Superior. I hear it roaring in the distance with a sound like giants crashing into each other. It is as if the icebergs along the shore are the lake's broad shoulders jostling against the frozen sand.

The Chippewa call Superior *Kitchi gami,* the big water. I have seen the Atlantic and the Pacific and neither is larger or better than this. Every time I come over a hill or around a bend and see it—rolling or calm, gray or blue, in any mood—I am home.

In our cabin we have electricity, but no running water. Instead we have cases of spring water imported from Canada, and a hole in the ice. We have a telephone but no television. We have a radio and it gets reception sometimes. We have two cats, two dogs, hundreds of books, and a Scrabble board. The closest grocery store is thirty miles away.

I am in no hurry to go to town; it has been nearly a month since I went. I don't want to disturb the chain of days I am threading together like pearls on a satin string. We need milk, stamps, dog food. Clean laundry. I know this, but it seems unimportant. It would be easy to earn the title of *hermit*.

These are our chores: light the fire, carry wood, spud the hole open in the ice, haul water up in buckets. Shovel now, wait for the mail. I wash my hair in a big white basin of lake water heated on top of the woodstove and do the dishes the same way. We play Scrabble or cribbage in the evening. We read. I write.

Sometimes my husband cooks dinner outside over a fire. One day he roasted pork, slowly, over cherry wood. The smell made me feel delirious and preoccupied and I couldn't think about anything else until it was done. That smell was the liveliest, most arresting thing about the day.

Sometimes I build a campfire on the beach and then scoop coffee grounds into cold water in a blue speckled pot and set the pot on a grate above the flames. It is the best coffee in the world, and makes me happier and more awake than any other.

It is quiet here. The lake is bigger than the town, and gets named on maps more often. Muskallonge means ugly fish in Chippewa. I like the practicality of that, and also the humor. The town is called Deer Park. There are many summer cabins, but only twenty-five permanent residents. There is one store open year-round, a quarter mile away. I buy candy bars there. Also canned vegetables, soup, potato chips, matches, and ice cream.

Mushers train their sled dogs here. We are north of the main snowmobile trails, so it is a good place to run dogs, quiet and empty. I have not seen this yet, but imagine it and wait: the dogs harnessed in a long string, running, the sled flying behind with the musher clinging to it, calling to the dogs. We pass a mushers' camp on our way to town when we go, a half circle of trailers and trucks. The mushers live in the trailers, the dogs in boxes in the backs of the trucks. There were men and women gathered around a fire in lawn chairs the last time we drove past, a little before noon on a Tuesday in January. Their lives looked even more rustic than mine. Their lives looked interesting.

Sometimes at night, after the shoveling is done, we light the kerosene lantern and walk slowly down the road in the dark. There is only the sound of our boots shuffling on the snow and the hishing noise the lantern makes. Sometimes a tree branch creaks loud in the woods on still, windless nights, and we stop and listen, and wonder. What made it creak? There is the smell of coldness and snow and burning kerosene. Our shadows are huge, our arms far above us, up over the treetops, brushing against the sky.

I always think about the people who were here before me, who might have loved it here as I do, and I am curious about them. I wish that I could meet them. Perhaps we would have a great deal in common. Life has always been harsh here, I think—harsh and beautiful and compelling. It is a place that inspires deep loyalty. More than once it has made me try to be more determined and more courageous than I really thought I could be.

We live poor here. We stay against great odds, our life in many ways like a white-knuckled, stubborn grasp. No one has yet been able to knock our fingers off the rock ledge of our life. I'd yearn to come back, if I had to leave. I'd dream of returning. I think my heart would break if I could not.

When you are old, perhaps you remember most clearly the best pieces, the magic pieces, of your life. I have a whole album of those, gathered here.

Standing on the ice of Muskallonge Lake under a full moon, with Orion striding over the eastern horizon, I watched a shooting star with a comet's tail blaze across the center of the sky, across the silent night.

One morning the sun rose over a jagged-toothed swamp, glowing brilliant orange and pink against the snow. I was the only person alive in the world, the only one watching morning come.

One evening thick fog hung above the ice, mysterious and ghostly. It flowed out of the woods to our north and hovered heavy, like a spirit, in front of us. It arrived just after sunset and stayed overnight. The next morning, the trees were sheathed in white, the fog frozen to their branches like the thickest spider webs draped down from the sky, or the finest lace.

All of the sunsets are glorious. Some are wild, some quiet. One night the bright yellow-orange ball of sun sank slowly into the trees along the lake's western shore, winking at me as it went, and I had a sudden, amazing flash of idea. If I ran across the ice, I could find the sun behind the jagged treetops. Somewhere deep in the cedar swamp, it rested in passionate splendor, glowing like fire and wisdom and magic and forever, its whereabouts a secret that only a few know—the firs and cedars, the rabbits and ravens, the owls and coyotes, the leatherleaf and bearberry. The sun does not travel away at night, does not vanish, does not light some other sphere. It isn't far away at all. It settles in the wild swamp across the lake to wait for morning.

There is something in the air here that clears the brain. This air can make you as happy as campfire coffee. At the edge of the big lake this morning, making snow angels with the dogs, I could taste happiness as sharp and clear as a chunk of ice in my mouth. I felt alive, awake. The dogs are shaggy, red-blonde retrievers with drooping smiles and an impossible expression of hopeful despair. They are loyal and stoic and foolish and dear. I sat up and they climbed into my lap to stare into my eyes, puzzled and endlessly patient.

Lake Superior in winter is breathtaking. It is gray, gun-metal water, floating drift ice, and icebergs with waves crashing against them, spraying over in huge, dramatic froths. I squatted on my heels, still and small, an Arctic shorebird, wings folded snug into my sides, watching the ice and water. I'd been transported suddenly, thousands of miles north to Hudson Bay or Alaska. I was seeing country no one else had ever seen, a pioneer.

The sky is always beautiful. Day or night, storm or calm, rain or sun, the sky is strong and amazing. Between Lake Superior and the sky, the north looms infinite, a great blue horizon. It is my great plains, my mountain ranges, my west. The sky and lake make everything large and wild. The air whispers *freedom*. That vast range of deep, cold blue water knows of wisdom and eternity.

In the summer I swim in the shallow water along the edge of Lake Superior, cold and thrilled and free. I am never, for any reason, anywhere, happier than this. Imagine. It is my entire life's purpose to see another summer here, to find at least one more morning to tumble in the waves. I need at least one more clear winter night, and another shooting star blazing across the center of the sky-above-the-lake.

Ellen Airgood *lives near Lake Superior with her husband and dogs and cats. Her essays have appeared in* Sierra, Simple Cooking, The Old Farmer's Almanac, *and* Traverse. *She is currently at work on a novel set in Michigan's Upper Peninsula.*

Evening Flight

Don Moser

The coastal marshes of northern Ohio compose the most biologically diverse portion of the state. Here on the edge of Lake Erie, dense insect populations and tall grasses attract reptiles, amphibians, small mammals, and spectacular crowds of resident and visiting birds.

It was almost time for the evening flight, and Jeff walked along the Lake Erie beach near the water's edge where the sand was hard, and the late sun threw a long shadow in front of him. A boy of eleven, he walked slowly, hands in his blue jeans pockets, his new tennis shoes leaving waffle-prints in the wet sand behind him. After a while he looked up and stopped. He saw Black Jack shuffle out of the sand dunes farther up the beach. Black Jack dropped his burlap sack of empty pop bottles on the sand and peered around. He saw Jeff and put his hand over his eyes to shade them from the low sun.

The boy and the old beachcomber stood on the sand looking at each other. Jeff took his hands from his pockets and rubbed them on his jeans. He was frightened. If Ken and Jimmy were with him he would not be afraid, but there was no one at all on the beach, nothing but the gulls curling over the water. Jeff didn't believe the stories he had heard about Black Jack putting children in the burlap sack and carrying them off to his shack down in the marsh. Jeff didn't believe that story or the others Ken's father had told him, but he was still afraid of the old man.

Black Jack kept peering at him from under his hand. Jeff thought, "I won't leave. I want to go to the bridge and see the birds. I'll just stand here and flip stones, and maybe he won't recognize me. If he comes down the beach I can run and I can beat him back to the park, and if he goes up the beach I can wait a while and go on to the bridge."

Jeff picked up a small flat stone from the sand and flipped it out on the water, using only his wrist. The stone sailed flat and bounced off the water and sailed and bounced again and again. The low sun turned the waves bright and silvery, and Jeff couldn't see the stone fly in the glare until it hit and made a splash of spray. He pretended to look for another stone then, watching the beachcomber out of the corner of his eye. He saw Black Jack pick up his sack of bottles again and sling it over his shoulder and go shuffling up the beach.

"He didn't recognize me," Jeff thought. "That's good. I can still go to the bridge now and see the flight."

Jeff stayed by the water's edge until Black Jack had gone farther up the beach, then followed slowly so that he wouldn't catch up. Black Jack moved along, taking his time, looking on the sand for empty soda-pop bottles and things bathers had left during the day. Jeff saw him lean over to pick something from the sand and put it in the burlap sack. "I wish he would hurry," Jeff thought. "I'll miss them if I don't get to the bridge soon."

After a while the old man passed the point where the path to the bridge came out of the dunes onto the beach, and when the boy reached it he ran in among the dunes, not afraid now that Black Jack couldn't see him. He ran along the faint sandy path, dodging twisted driftwood logs until he reached the grass meadow that skirted the marsh. He followed the meadow to the line of willow trees and went down among them, stooping low under the heavy-hanging branches. He parted the branches and came out onto the old wooden footbridge that crossed a neck of the marsh.

Jeff walked onto the bridge and climbed up on the wide handrail and sat on it, swinging his legs over the dark water. "I'm in time," he thought. "They haven't started yet." He looked out across the low dunes to the lake lying like hammered silver in the sun. "The flight won't start until the sun is almost on the water," he thought. He pushed his brown hair back from his eyes and watched the swallows spinning over the marsh, and thought about how he had first found the bridge and watched the evening flight.

Two weeks before, Jeff had moved from the city to the little shore village on the lake. A few evenings ago his new friends, Ken and Jimmy, asked him to go to the beach with them. Jeff's mother didn't want him to go because of the things she had heard about the old man who lived in the marsh and prowled the beach in the evening.

"He's filthy," she said. "I saw him down at Morrow's grocery—he'd brought in a sack of bottles to get the deposit refunds. He's the filthiest thing I've ever seen, and I don't want you to go near that man." But Jeff's father said that he could go if he was careful.

So he and Ken and Jimmy went to the beach, and they saw Black Jack there and teased him. After they ran away from him, they walked along the water's edge looking for stones and shells. Moving ahead, Ken picked up something from the sand, then called for them to come look at it. He held a small piece of driftwood, smoothed and shaped by the waves so that it looked like a knife—like a pirate's dagger. Jeff wanted the dagger, but Ken said that he was going to sand it and paint it silver like a real dagger. And when they walked back down the beach, Ken wore it stuck in his belt, draping his hand carelessly over the hilt.

The next night Jeff went back to the beach to see if he could find another. Ken and Jimmy had gone to the movies, so he went alone. He walked up the beach for a long way, much farther than they had gone the night before, and he watched the sand closely for a piece of driftwood shaped like a dagger, but he found nothing. Then he came upon the faint path leading back through the dunes, and wondering where it led, he followed it to the bridge.

He had sat on the rail, just as now, and then the flight began, with all the world yellow in the sunset and the small birds flying in thousands up the marsh. He watched it until dusk, and he had never seen anything like it before. It was better than African movies, better than circuses, better than anything.

Something dimpled the water of the marsh, and a ring swelled out across the dark smooth surface and rippled against cattail stems. Jeff wondered what had done it. Then a rustling sound came from the willows. Jeff looked at the green band of trees and stiffened.

Black Jack shuffled out of the willows onto the bridge. The burlap sack of bottles clinked as he set it on the footboards. Black Jack peered down the bridge and saw Jeff. "Hello, boy," he said. His voice was hard.

Jeff sat frozen still on the rail and didn't answer. He stared at Black Jack. The old man's face was red, with wrinkles black-lined with dirt. His long gray hair was matted over his ears and hung down from beneath his smashed hat. Red eyes looked out from under thick gray eyebrows. He wore baggy trousers and a dark and greasy suit coat ripped at the shoulder. He had old and calloused hands. Black Jack leaned against the rail and looked down the marsh.

Jeff sat unmoving on the rail. "I wonder if I ought to run?" he thought. But if he ran down to the other end of the bridge he would come out into the marshes, and he was afraid he would get lost or fall into the quicksand Ken said was there. And he couldn't get to the beach end of the bridge without passing Black Jack. He was afraid of the old man, but he didn't want to leave and miss the flight. "Maybe he won't know me," Jeff thought. "I hope he doesn't remember me."

They had teased Black Jack when he came shuffling along the sand looking for bottles. They ran up the beach before him and found some bottles by a burned out campfire. They waited until the old man got almost to them, then they threw the bottles far out into the waves. Jeff wanted to stop them, but Ken ran near the old man and screamed at him, "You're a tramp! You're a dirty tramp!" Then Ken pulled out his slingshot and picked up a pebble from the sand and snapped it away. It hit Black Jack in the shoulder, and he dropped the sack of bottles and started to chase Ken, half running, half shuffling in the soft sand. They all ran then, down the long beach near the water's edge until the old man was just a small black shape behind them.

Suddenly Black Jack stepped away from the bridge rail and pointed out toward the lake.

"Look there," he said.

Jeff looked up. Two specks cracked down over the marsh and flashed high above the bridge. At the east end of the marsh the ducks banked and turned and came back low over the bridge, wings straining against the air, heads out straight on long necks. They slid out across the bright water of the lake into the sun. The boy and the old man shaded their eyes with their hands and watched them until they were gone.

"Them's mallards," Black Jack said.

"I know it," Jeff lied. "Anybody knows mallards."

Black Jack took off his hat and ran his hand through his matted gray hair. Then he looked at Jeff, who was staring at him with wide eyes.

"You ever been here before, boy?"

"Sure, I've been here lots of times. I've been all through these marshes."

It was only the third time he had been there. There was the first night and then last night when he had asked his father to go with him to the bridge. He tried to tell his father about the flight, but his father was reading the paper, and he said he was too tired to walk all that way down the beach. "Why don't you take Kenneth?" his father said. "And you be careful about that old tramp who lives down there in the marsh. I don't want you going near him." Jeff didn't want to take Ken somehow. He didn't think Ken would like the place he had found, but he did take him, finally.

"Hey, boy," Black Jack said, "ain't you one of them kids who was pestering me the other night?" Jeff sat stiffly on the rail and looked at the old man's calloused hands and the big burlap sack curled on the footboards. "Ain't you one of them kids?"

"No. I never bothered you. I've never seen you before."

Black Jack shuffled a few steps closer and peered at the boy with his small red eyes. Jeff gripped the rail and bit down on his lip. "Do you know that tow-headed kid? Ken, his name is."

"No. No, I don't know him."

"Well, that kid's no good. I better not ever get my hands on him. He'll be sorry if I do."

Black Jack rubbed his hands on his dirty trousers and leaned against the rail again.

Jeff relaxed his grip on the rail and sucked in a deep breath. When he had brought Ken to the marsh the night before to show him the flight, Ken stamped on the bridge and shook it and tried to break off a section of the rail, and Jeff began to wish that he had come alone. Later, after the flight began, Jeff looked over at Ken standing spread-legged with his slingshot pulled back the length of his arm. "Hey!" Jeff cried, but the sling snapped and one of the birds dropped from the flock and fell softly onto the water. The small brown bird floated slowly down beneath them with its still wings stretched out on the smooth water and its head turned sideways on the neck, one veiled eye gazing up at them.

"Here," Ken said, holding out the sling. "You want to get one?"

"No." Jeff watched the dead bird swing in slow circles on the water. "Don't shoot any more, all right?"

And Ken didn't shoot any more, but the evening was spoiled for Jeff, so this night he had come to the bridge alone.

Black Jack was fumbling in the deep pockets of his old coat. He brought out something wrapped in brown paper. He sloughed the paper off and took out a thick meat sandwich. He broke it in two and held one of the halves toward Jeff. "You want a piece of samwich, boy?"

"No, thank you," Jeff said. "I'm not hungry."

The old man shrugged. He ate one of the halves of the sandwich, stuffing it into his mouth and licking his fingers afterward. Then he took a chunk of the meat from the other half and dropped it into the water below the bridge. The water swirled and splashed and the meat was gone. Jeff stared at the rippling water. Black Jack looked at him and grinned.

"What was it?" Jeff whispered.

"Bass," Black Jack said. "There's big 'uns in here. Watch now." He broke another piece from the sandwich and dropped it into the water. The swirl and splash again, and the meat was gone. "If you stand right here above 'em," he said, "you can see 'em in the water."

Jeff hesitated, then climbed down from the rail and walked slowly down the bridge. A few feet from the old man he stopped and looked over the rail. His mouth opened in surprise. Two heavy dark shapes coasted in slow circles in the brown water below him. Black Jack dropped another piece of meat. Jeff saw one of the shapes circle near the floating meat, saw the muscle-banded tail snap and the sudden flash and swirl of the strike. Black Jack dropped another piece and this time the other fish struck. Jeff stood on the bottom rail and leaned out to watch the two long shadows cruising in the dark water.

"Hey!" Black Jack said. "You be careful you don't fall in there, boy." He held out the rest of the sandwich toward Jeff. "Here, boy. You want to feed 'em some?"

"No." Jeff stepped down from the rail. "They aren't any-thing. They're just old fish."

He moved back down the bridge a few feet and leaned against the rail and looked out across the dunes to the lake. The sun almost touched the waves. The flight would begin soon, Jeff thought. He wished that Black Jack would leave. If he stayed he would spoil it.

"If you find something really nice," the boy thought, "you want to tell somebody. You want somebody to see it with you and talk about it a little bit afterward. But if you do tell some-body, they either don't come, like my father; or they spoil it, like Ken, so it's better not to tell anybody and just watch it by yourself."

Black Jack scratched himself. "Birds'll start coming up the marsh pretty soon now," he said. "The sun is almost on the water, so they'll start pretty soon, and you never seen so many birds."

"There's not so many," Jeff said. "I've been here lots of times. This place isn't much."

"Well, maybe it's not," the old man said. "I always thought this was a pretty nice place, but I guess there's plenty of places I ain't ever been."

"Why can't he leave and not spoil it?" Jeff thought. He re-membered some of the things that his father and Ken's father had said about Black Jack. Ken's father said that he was a worthless old tramp, and the sheriff should get rid of him be-cause the villagers didn't like to let their children go down to the beach alone with him always prowling around.

Black Jack took a dark old pipe from the pocket of his coat and dipped it full from a cracked leather tobacco pouch. He struck a big wooden match on the rail and lit the pipe. He puffed out smoke, then suddenly pointed down the marsh with his pipe stem.

"Here they come, boy. Here come the first of them."

Jeff looked down the marsh and saw a group of specks grow into flying birds and whir in across the water. They passed low on straining wings over the man and the boy on the bridge.

Another flock spun out of the cattails and then another and another. The low sun cut across the marsh, and the world of the marsh turned butter-yellow in the evening light. The north wind came in from the lake and moved in the sweeping branches of the willows and rustled them, and the tall poplars standing down the marsh spun their silver leaves in the sunset. The flocks of small brown birds came up out of the cattails and up out of the marshland, and they filled the air with the rush of their soft wings and the high, thin sound of their voices. The flocks became larger and joined together and joined again and passed in streaming hundreds above the bridge.

The old man moved down the bridge and leaned against the rail at Jeff's side. The boy looked at him, then looked back to the flight.

"What are they?"

"Red-wings," the old man said. "I call 'em that, but it don't matter much what the name is."

"But they are brown," the boy said. "The wings aren't red at all."

"Them is just the mother birds. The mothers and the young 'uns. The fathers got red on the wings, but they left already. Gone South for the winter. These'll go too, pretty soon now." He pointed into the streaming flocks with his pipe stem.

"Watch them, boy," he said. "Watch them, how they race the sun."

Jeff looked up again. There were flocks no longer, just a great river of flying birds thrumming up out of the marsh and whirring over the bridge on soft dark wings. Jeff sat on the rail

with his legs over the brown water and smelled the strong, rich smell of the old man's pipe, and he saw the swallows cutting and skimming over the smooth water and whisking through the cattail clumps. He watched a pair of teal drop from high against a tower of clouds on fire in sunset and rifle in across the lake and over evening-yellow dunes and all the yellow burlap land of cattails and marsh grasses. And above the lake gulls turned on long, bent wings against the sun and dropped to the glittering waves.

The sun was almost gone behind the edge of the water and the marsh turned from yellow into gray and only the tall poplars glittered yellow and silver down the last seconds of the day. And the rushing stream above him became flocks again, and the flocks grew smaller and smaller as they strained up out of the dusk. The gray line of night moved up the yellow and silver of the poplars and then it reached the top and the yellow and silver were gone and out across the lake the sun was gone and in the air the birds were gone, and the air was empty and quiet.

The boy and the old man on the bridge were silent. The old man drew on his pipe and blew the smoke out into the air; the boy swung his legs and looked down at the water below them.

"I wonder where they all go?" he said.

"To find some place to sleep, some place to spend the night," the old man said. "I don't know where they go, exactly, but I like to watch them here at evening when they fly the marsh. Look there, boy. There's the first bat. You see him?"

Jeff saw the bat spin and turn above the cattails on quick wings. "He's fast," Jeff said. "I didn't know they were so fast. I've never seen one before."

They stayed on the bridge for a while, watching the bat; then the old man knocked out his pipe against the rail.

"Be dark pretty soon, boy. You want to walk back down the beach with me?"

Jeff looked at the old man and hesitated for a moment. Then, "No," he said. "I don't go home along the beach. I go across the bridge and through the marshes. I don't care about the dark anyway."

"All right, boy. If you can find your way. Good night now."

The old man shuffled back down the bridge and picked up his clinking sack of bottles, then went down into the willows and was gone. Jeff sat on the rail with his chin in his hands and looked down at the water. He sat there for a while, and then he climbed down and went off the bridge and through the willows. He crossed the meadow and went in among the dunes. He walked slowly along the path, his hands jammed down in his pockets. When he reached the beach he saw something dark and shiny half buried in the sand. He stopped and kicked at it with his tennis shoe, then reached down and picked it up. He held it in his hand and stood there looking at it for a long time, and then he looked up, and he ran, ran down the long beach in the dusk after the small dark figure ahead of him, holding the bottle to his chest.

Born and raised in Cleveland, Ohio, **Don Moser** *attended Ohio University and Stanford University. He spent several summers working as a seasonal ranger in the Olympics and the Grand Tetons where, he says, his greatest accomplishment was saving a drowning moose. The author of many books and articles, he recently retired from more than twenty years as editor in chief of* Smithsonian *magazine.*

Prairie after Rain

MARCIA LIPSON

Dandelion light turns silver
as Nellie bounds from the river,
shaking her fur and scaring deer
who skitter to the cover of the oak trees,
while doves settle on heaps of flowerpots
the gardener, ignoring the small things,
has tossed aside.

Marcia Lipson *was a professor of twentieth-century literature at Hunter College in New York and a widely published poet.*

Hay Field Bestiary

DAVID KLINE

Although the Great North American Prairie region reaches its eastern limit in Illinois, pockets of prairie dot parts of Indiana, Michigan, and Ohio. In this essay from his book, Scratching the Woodchuck, *Ohio farmer David Kline illuminates the many similarities between a midwestern hay field and the wild, open prairie.*

It always surprises me how quickly hay fields abound with new life once regrowth begins in the spring. Migrant birds arrive, pair off, and begin nesting. Mammals move in from the edges. Soon the fields ring with bird song and bustle with the activities of all the new inhabitants.

To me, a mixed grass-and-legume hay field is an eastern version of the lush midwestern prairie. Many of the animals, birds, and insects here are the same as those inhabiting native prairies. Grassland birds, unlike their woodland cousins, often sing on the wing. And the songs of some, like the meadowlark and bobolink, are loud enough to carry well on the wind and across the great distances of open spaces. Unfortunately, the field's richness of life peaks around mid-June, right at the time the hay needs to be cut.

I was cutting the first round of hay when a red fox left the field and headed for the security of the fencerow. I was happy to see the fox, a pup, which means a litter was raised nearby. About a month ago I had found a partially eaten muskrat at the edge of the hay field, a killing that looked like the work of a family of red foxes. The pair of foxes whose tracks crisscrossed the fields in last winter's snow apparently decided to stay and raise their family. Along the fence line there are at least a dozen woodchuck burrows; any one could be the home of the foxes.

I greatly admire the red fox, for its grace and beauty and its ability to survive in the proximity of humans. A family of red foxes on the farm makes it a better place to live.

Soon after I saw the fox several half-grown cottontail rabbits left the hay field, going in the opposite direction of the fox. The fox may have been stalking the rabbits when I flushed it out. Indeed, the field is a premier stalking arena: the shrew stalks the beetles and earthworms; the weasel stalks the shrew; the fox stalks the voles and cottontails; the red-tailed hawk watches for weasels, voles, cottontails, and shrews; the crow searches for the eggs and young of red-winged blackbirds—as does the black rat snake—and the Cooper's hawk darts out from the cover of the woods to snatch a bobolink or redwing or horned lark. The skilled eat. Fortunately, there is an abundance of life.

One evening I saw a weasel out for an early hunt. It was headed my way, so I remained motionless. Every few lopes it would stop and sniff the air (did it smell a mouse or was it me?) but then kept coming closer. The weasel's back was grayish brown and the underside white. It was slender and only around ten inches long, and it ran humpbacked. I saw spots of blood on its nose as it passed between my legs.

The red-winged blackbirds nest early and most of their young are already flying. Likewise with the savannah sparrows: their young are everywhere, clinging to stalks of weeds and grass. But the bobolinks are late again; I haven't seen any flying young.

Last evening as I was coming home from raking hay in our far field, I passed the uncut mixed hay field. It was just before sunset, at the time the bobolinks are at their finest, and I counted sixteen males zigzagging across the field, chasing mates and competitors, and singing their lively songs. I paused to listen and to watch the birds, and tried to envision what it must have

been like when the first Europeans saw the vast expanse of the American prairie—a band of grass six hundred miles across and extending a thousand miles from north to south. How many millions of bobolinks were in those virgin grasslands?

We'll wait to cut that field. Give the bobolinks a week, and their young may be flying.

Another animal I saw while mowing hay this week was a white-tailed deer. It had bedded down along the edge of the field, but when I approached it spooked and left. The deer, a buck with antlers in velvet, was wearing its reddish-brown summer coat, so different from the drab gray of winter.

Of course, there are the usual woodchucks in the hay field. In fact, without the woodchucks there would be less life altogether in the hay field. The red foxes, for one, wouldn't have raised their family here if it hadn't been for the woodchuck's burrows. The cottontails and weasels also use the burrows. Even the pair of bobwhite quail that lives in the hay field may use the woodchuck's den in the wintertime to escape freezing rains. For many grassland creatures, the woodchuck's burrows are crucial for surviving the perils of predation and fierce weather. Long live the grizzled hay-eating rodents.

David Kline *is a farmer and the author of* Scratching the Woodchuck: Nature on an Amish Farm.

Mush Again

Lisa Wheeler

In Michigan
it's mush again,
slick and sleety slush again,
and folks are in
a rush again
to shovel, salt, and plow.

If Michigan
could wish again,
it wouldn't snow like this again
at least not here
in Michigan,
where flakes are falling now.

Lisa Wheeler—*author of twelve picture books (among them* Sixteen Cows, Sailor Moo: Cow at Sea, *and* Porcupining: A Prickly Love Story), *one poetry book (*Wool Gathering), *and the* Fitch & Chip Ready-to-Read series for Simon & Schuster—*has seen lots of slushy, mushy snow in her southeast Michigan neighborhood. "The salt trucks are out before the first flake hits the ground. The result? Slush!"*

Saving Lake Erie

GRETCHEN WOELFLE

To Karen Reed Kearns

People who live beside the Great Lakes reap many benefits from them—stunning views, fresh fish, places to swim and sail, and more. Many residents recognize, too, that with these benefits comes a responsibility to take care of the lakes and the plants and animals that live within them.

When you grow up on Lake Erie you get the wrong idea about lakes. You think they are huge. You think all lakes are so big that you can't see land when you look across or up and down the lake. You think all lakes have waves that are taller than you are, big enough to knock you down if you're not careful.

I grew up on Lake Erie in Dunkirk, New York, a small town south of Buffalo. It was the only lake I knew until I went to camp on Bear Lake. I could see all the edges of Bear Lake without binoculars. We even swam across the lake—all of half a mile—on Saturday afternoons. Then I realized that there are lakes and there are Great Lakes!

Lake Erie isn't as big as the three Great Lakes to the west (Huron, Michigan, and Superior), and it has less water than smaller Lake Ontario to the east. Lake Erie is the shallowest lake of the five. That helps to make it the warmest Great Lake in the summer.

When I was growing up, summer meant no school, juicy strawberries, and fresh corn from local farm stands. It meant picnics with my grandparents at the Point every Sunday. But most of all it meant swimming in Lake Erie. When I was a toddler, I got knocked over by a big wave and saved by my grandfather who jumped in after me with all his clothes on. I heard the story so many times that I think I remember tumbling over in the waves and choking on the water that filled my mouth and nose. I learned to swim a couple of years later—in a sheltered cove where the waves weren't very big.

We swam nearly every day in the summer. This was in the 1950s in small-town, middle-class New York, where most mothers stayed home and kept house. They sat and watched us kids from the beach. My mother was an expert at this, for she'd been a lifeguard at the same beach in high school. Day by day we acquired bright red sunburns, then dark brown tans. No one used sunscreen back then.

When the lake was calm, we had "chicken fights," sitting on each other's shoulders, trying to knock another person into the water. We floated on our backs and turned somersaults underwater. We swam out over our heads to the sandbar where suddenly the water was only knee-deep. We felt like giants as we waved to our mothers far away on the beach. When the waves were high we dove under them or tumbled through them. But we were sternly warned about the undertow. My friend Karen had nightmares of it dragging her underwater all the way to Canada.

Our fathers worked during the day. But in the evenings and

on weekends, they fished in their out-
board motorboats, bringing back lines
of blue pike, walleyes, and whitefish
to fry in batter and eat with
tartar sauce. If our
mothers didn't feel
like cooking on Friday
nights, a dozen churches or
social clubs in town offered fish
dinners for a dollar or two.

The winter brought another kind of fun. Because Lake
Erie is so shallow, it freezes every winter. Sometimes it would
freeze all the way to Canada. Some parts close to shore were
smooth enough to skate on. But the real treat the lake gave us
was huge ice mounds—at least they seemed huge to us. The
wind and waves pushed together these steep, lumpy slabs of
ice, and they were perfect for sleds we called flying saucers.
The ice mounds were especially exciting because they were
so dangerous. Our parents, principals, and even the local
newspapers warned us *not* to play on the ice mounds. Patches
of thin ice could give way. The ice mounds could split apart
and swallow us up. We would die in the frigid water in no
time at all.

I went out on the ice mounds to sled only with my parents.
But Karen, who lived right by the lake, went out there with just
her friend Bobby when they were about five years old. Bobby
fell through the ice and Karen decided to help him by jumping
in herself! They were in shallow water, but they couldn't climb
out. Karen's dog, Sherry, had more sense than either of the
children. Just like Lassie, the 1950s TV dog, Sherry ran home
and barked until Karen's mother came to rescue the two cold,

wet children. Only Karen's red mittens were lost. Once they got wet, they'd frozen to the ice.

Winter storms often changed the shape of the beaches. Every spring they were wider or narrower, or sandier or rockier than they'd been the summer before. But the shape of the beach didn't matter much to us, as we waited for the water to warm up in June.

Several times every summer we could smell the beach before we got there. The "seaweed" had returned. It wasn't really seaweed, but thick, slimy green algae that coated the beach and the shallows of the lake. We held our noses as we waded through the mucky mess, here and there avoiding a floating dead fish, until we got beyond the algae to clear water where we could swim. In a few days, the algae would drift to the beach and rot, smelling even worse. Finally the stinky stuff went away and the lake became "clean" again.

But Lake Erie wasn't really clean. On its eastern tip stood Buffalo, New York; to the west lay Cleveland and Toledo, Ohio; to the north lay Detroit, Michigan—all of them major industrial centers. Steel, auto, and tire plants, and power-generating stations all poured leftover chemicals into Lake Erie, or into rivers that flowed to the lake. The cities released untreated sewage water too. Those dead fish that stared up at us gave us a warning about the entire lake ecosystem.

After I moved away from Lake Erie in 1959, things got even worse. I returned to Dunkirk for a visit in 1971, and the beaches were closed. The lake was too polluted for people to swim, and too polluted for most fish to live. Barry Commoner, a famous ecologist, declared that year that "the most blatant example of the environmental crisis in the United States is Lake Erie."

No one had talked about the "environment" in the 1950s. But by 1971, people couldn't ignore problems like Lake Erie, and the environmental movement came to life. Some people who lived near the lake became community activists. They listened to the scientists who studied Lake Erie, then took those studies to their lawmakers. In 1972, Canada and the United States passed joint legislation that laid out strict rules about what could and could not be dumped in the lakes. New sewage treatment plants were ordered for factories, towns, and cities. Many toxic chemicals were removed or transformed into harmless compounds before they entered the lake.

The major culprit behind Lake Erie's pollution was phosphorus. This chemical acts as a fertilizer in your garden and in a lake. Large amounts of phosphorus fed those green, slimy, smelly algae that invaded our beach every summer. When the algae died and sank to the bottom of the lake, they were eaten by billions of tiny bacteria that used up oxygen. Without oxygen, fish, plants, and other lake life died. The popular blue pike became extinct in Lake Erie.

Many factories produced phosphorus as a waste product. Farmers used phosphorus to fertilize crops, and runoff from the fields emptied into the lake. Cities didn't "treat" their sewage. They only allowed particles to settle out, and sent the rest of it, untreated, back into the lake. Laundry day at home added to the problem. Our mothers, wanting our clothes to be whiter than white, used detergents with large amounts of phosphorus. Factories, farms, and everyday life—who thought they could come so close to killing a Great Lake?

Cleaned-up industries, sewage treatment plants, laundry detergents without phosphorus, and nature's remarkable power to heal itself all helped to bring the lake back to life. It was a slow process, but by the mid-1980s, phosphorus discharges were way down, oxygen levels rose, algae blooms occurred only rarely, and fish began to thrive again in Lake Erie.

A few years ago I drove through my hometown with my daughters and we all swam in Lake Erie. The water was clear and kids waved to their mothers from the sand bar, just as I remembered. That same year, the Great Lakes states passed laws to limit the discharge of twenty-two more toxins into the lakes.

Today, scientists are pleased with the water quality in the lake. The treatment plants are in place and operating efficiently. But new dangers to Lake Erie now come from exotic species from distant ecosystems, such as ruffe and goby fish, Asiatic clams, and tiny zooplankton called spiny water fleas. The worst of these exotic invaders are zebra mussels. Riding on a ship from northern Europe, they traveled through the St. Lawrence Seaway into the Great Lakes. Billions of them have upset the ecological balance, nearly driving Lake Erie clams into extinction. And so community activists, scientists, and lawmakers are still hard at work, for they appreciate more than ever the lake they almost lost.

Members of one threatened species, Lake Erie fisherfolk—men and women—have returned in droves. A fishing contest for the biggest walleye, held in Dunkirk every summer, attracts thousands of amateurs and professionals who compete for the grand prize of $50,000. A big walleye weighs eight to ten pounds. A prize-winner might weigh eleven pounds. At nearly $5,000 a pound, that's a valuable fish. But everyone who fishes or swims or sits on the beach to watch the sun set over Lake Erie has won a prize that's even more valuable—a truly great lake.

Gretchen Woelfle *grew up in Dunkirk, New York, and now lives in Los Angeles, California. She writes fiction and nonfiction for children of all ages and travels around the country and the world to get ideas for her stories.*

The Copper Beech

MARIE HOWE

Immense, entirely itself,
it wore that yard like a dress,

with limbs low enough for me to enter it
and climb the crooked ladder to where

I could lean against the trunk and practice being alone.

One day, I heard the sound before I saw it, rain fell
darkening the sidewalk.

Sitting close to the center, not very high in the branches,
I heard it hitting the high leaves, and I was happy,

watching it happen without it happening to me.

Marie Howe *grew up in Rochester, New York, the eldest daughter
among nine siblings. Her poems have appeared in many magazines
and in her own poetry collections, including* The Good Thief *and*
What the Living Do.

A Mighty Fortress

ALDO LEOPOLD

For the majority of timbercutters, the most valued trees in the forest are those that are tall, healthy, and unmarred by bumps and burls. But a forest is more than a place for growing timber; it's also a home and a pantry for animals—many of whom think very highly of diseased, rotted, and fallen trees.

Every farm woodland, in addition to yielding lumber, fuel, and posts, should provide its owner a liberal education. This crop of wisdom never fails, but it is not always harvested. I here record some of the many lessons I have learned in my own woods.

Soon after I bought the woods a decade ago, I realized that I had bought almost as many tree diseases as I had trees. My woodlot is riddled by all the ailments wood is heir to. I began to wish that Noah, when he loaded up the Ark, had left the tree diseases behind. But it soon became clear that these same diseases made my woodlot a mighty fortress, unequaled in the whole county.

My woods is headquarters for a family of coons; few of my neighbors have any. One Sunday in November, after a new snow, I learned why. The fresh track of a coon-hunter and his hound led up to a half-uprooted maple, under which one of my coons had taken refuge. The frozen snarl of roots and earth was too rocky to chop and too tough to dig; the holes under the roots were too numerous to smoke out. The hunter had quit coonless because a fungus disease had weakened the roots of the maple. The tree, half tipped over by a storm, offers an impregnable fortress for coondom. Without this "bombproof" shelter, my seed stock of coons would be cleaned out by hunters each year.

My woods houses a dozen ruffed grouse, but during periods of deep snow my grouse shift to my neighbor's woods, where there is better cover. However, I always retain as many grouse as I have oaks wind-thrown by summer storms. These summer windfalls keep their dried leaves, and during snows each such windfall harbors a grouse. The droppings show that each grouse roosts, feeds, and loafs for the duration of the storm within the narrow confines of his leafy camouflage, safe from wind, owl, fox, and hunter. The cured oak leaves not only serve as cover, but for some curious reason, are relished as food by the grouse.

These oak windfalls are, of course, diseased trees. Without disease, few oaks would break off, and hence few grouse would have down tops to hide in.

Diseased oaks also provide another apparently delectable grouse food: oak galls. A gall is a diseased growth of new twigs that have been stung by a gall-wasp while tender and succulent. In October my grouse are often stuffed with oak galls.

Each year the wild bees load up one of my hollow oaks with

combs, and each year trespassing honey-hunters harvest the honey before I do. This is partly because they are more skillful than I am in "lining up" the bee trees, and partly because they use nets, and hence are able to work before the bees become dormant in fall. But for heart-rots, there would be no hollow oaks to furnish wild bees with oaken hives.

During high years of the cycle, there is a plague of rabbits in my woods. They eat the bark and twigs off almost every kind of tree or bush I am trying to encourage, and ignore almost every kind I should like to have less of. (When the rabbit-hunter plants himself a grove of pines or an orchard, the rabbit somehow ceases to be a game animal and becomes a pest instead.)

The rabbit, despite his omnivorous appetite, is an epicure in some respects. He always prefers a hand-planted pine, maple, apple, or wahoo to a wild one. He also insists that certain salads be preconditioned before he deigns to eat them. Thus he spurns red dogwood until it is attacked by oyster-shell scale, after which the bark becomes a delicacy to be eagerly devoured by all the rabbits in the neighborhood.

A flock of a dozen chickadees spends the year in my woods. In winter, when we are harvesting diseased or dead trees for our fuel wood, the ring of the axe is dinner gong for the chickadee tribe. They hang in the offing waiting for the tree to fall, offering pert commentary on the slowness of our labor. When the tree at last is down, and the wedges begin to open up its contents, the chickadees draw up their white napkins and fall to. Every slab of dead bark is, to them, a treasury of eggs, larvae, and cocoons. For them every ant-tunneled heart-wood bulges with milk and honey. We often stand a fresh split against a nearby tree just to see the greedy chicks mop up the ant-eggs. It lightens our labor to know that they, as well as we, derive aid and comfort from the fragrant riches of newly split oak.

But for diseases and insect pests, there would likely be no food in these trees, and hence no chickadees to add cheer to my woods in winter.

Many other kinds of wildlife depend on tree diseases. My pileated woodpeckers chisel living pines, to extract fat grubs from the diseased heartwood. My barred owls find surcease from crows and jays in the hollow heart of an old basswood; but for this diseased tree their sundown serenade would probably be silenced. My wood ducks nest in hollow trees; every June brings its brood of downy ducklings to my woodland slough. All squirrels depend, for permanent dens, on a delicately balanced equilibrium between a rotting cavity and the scar tissue with which the tree attempts to close the wound. The squirrels referee the contest by gnawing out the scar tissue when it begins unduly to shrink the amplitude of their front door.

The real jewel of my disease-ridden woodlot is the prothonotary warbler. He nests in an old woodpecker hole, or other small cavity, in a dead snag overhanging

water. The flash of his gold-and-blue plumage amid the dank decay of the June woods is in itself proof that dead trees are transmuted into living animals, and vice versa. When you doubt the wisdom of this arrangement, take a look at the prothonotary.

Born in Iowa in 1887, **Aldo Leopold** *lived most of his life in Wisconsin where he worked for the Forest Service and the University of Wisconsin. Although he never claimed to be a nature writer in his time, his book* A Sand County Almanac *became a classic of nature writing after his death and is considered an essential text in environmental studies and environmental ethics.*

The Glowing Brown Snails of Blueberry Lake

Freya Manfred

The first time I dived under water
and opened my eyes near shore
I saw the glowing brown snails
of Blueberry Lake.
Shaggy black mussels too,
that pumped themselves shut
when I touched their soft lips.
And old sticks, soggy and twisted,
wriggling like water snakes
through rust-soft, leathery reeds.
And acorns, worn creamy white
in the constant waves, caught
between rocks and pebbles:
pink, brown, green, and blue.
And one gray stone
with the black and white print
of a maple leaf
stamped on it forever
by the press of winter ice.

Freya Manfred *is a poet who lives near Pequot Lakes, Minnesota. She is the author of a book of poetry entitled* American Roads, *a chapbook called* Flesh and Blood, *and a literary memoir entitled* Frederick Manfred: A Daughter Remembers.

Leaves

SARA ST. ANTOINE

In southeastern Michigan, flat to rolling farmland lies broken up by high-ways and towns and scattered woodlands. Although the terrain may seem bland and unremarkable to outsiders, local residents often take a different view.

I met Jake Peterson in the first week of eleventh grade. It was a hazy and humid Michigan afternoon—the season's last warm breath before fall set in—and both of us were trying to get a cold drink from the water fountain outside the high school.

"You run cross country?" he asked me, eyeing my sweaty T-shirt and well-worn running shoes.

"Just track, really," I told him. "But I train with the cross-country team sometimes in the fall."

"Don't you run out of country to cross?" he asked.

I looked at him, puzzled.

He explained that he had just moved to Ann Arbor from Missoula, Montana. It was a lot drier there, he said. There was a lot more land and a lot more sky.

"Hang in there," I told him as I jogged off to find the other runners. "Autumn is outstanding here."

Three days later, the temperature fell to sixty-five and the humidity blew away. I kept my eye out for Jake at school, wanting to know if he was happier now. But I never crossed his path.

"I met this sort of cute guy from Montana last week," I told my friend Delia the next Saturday afternoon. We were in her backyard, taking care of her younger brothers while her parents attended the University of Michigan football game.

"And?"

"And he said Ann Arbor was crowded and humid. He said it felt tame."

Delia tilted back her head and gazed up at the blue sky framed by the green leaves of a Norway maple. A cool breeze blew across our faces, and in the distance we could hear the drumbeat of the Michigan marching band doing its half-time routine. "He sounds crazy," she said. "It's perfect here."

Delia, I knew, could be exuberant about pot holes. But I still thought she was right.

My affection for Ann Arbor was a year-round habit. I loved early morning summer runs through Gallup Park, the mist slowly lifting up off the river to reveal another day. I loved walking under the trees in the Arboretum each spring after the hatch of their impossibly new, chartreuse leaves. I loved Park Washtenaw in winter, the tall brown grasses bent under the weight of the fallen snow. And I loved every part of town in autumn—the tree-lined streets, the football stadium, the farmer's market, the orchards.

Growing up, I'd been able to satisfy all my cravings for adventure without venturing far from home. My neighborhood may have looked like an ordered assemblage of suburban houses and lawns on the surface, but as kids we knew that there were still untamed places on the margins, and that they belonged to us.

Miss Tilden, the elderly neighbor who once lived across the street, knew all about this other world. She watched us making forts under the blue spruce, racing behind the juniper bushes, tunneling through piles of musty leaves.

"If you're out sometime and you see a plant that looks like this," she said, showing me a picture of a white flower called a trillium in one of her books, "would you let me know?"

"But don't you know where everything is?" I asked her. Miss Tilden knew the names of all the wildflowers and trees and birds in the neighborhood. She let a tangle of bushes grow on part of her yard so the birds would have places to feed and nest.

"I know about some things, Liza," she said. "But I don't sneak into as many scruffy places as you do."

The following Monday, Jake transferred into my fifth-period biology class. I introduced him to Delia right before Mr. Hanson started his lecture on the carbon cycle.

"Are you loving Ann Arbor yet?" Delia asked him, as if she expected nothing but a resounding "yes!" in reply.

Mr. Hanson cleared his throat and pointed to a picture of dead animals and rotted logs on the blackboard.

"It's OK," Jake said with a shrug.

Mr. Hanson started to explain how carbon is transferred from dead organic matter into the soil with the help of decomposers, like earthworms and beetles. I tried to concentrate, but it was hard for rotting carcasses to hold my attention. There were tiny burrs clinging to the fuzz of Jake's fleece jacket, stowaways from a distant habitat.

After class, Delia told me she thought Jake needed help getting to know Ann Arbor. Delia had always been braver than I, and I counted on her for most of my social adventures. "Here's what we'll do. Next week, we'll rent canoes and paddle down the Huron River. The next week, frisbee and a picnic in the Arb. By the next week, the apple orchards should be ready for picking. We'll take him to Wiard's or the Dexter Cider Mill. Once he tastes real cinnamon-covered cider donuts, forget it—he'll be hooked."

"On Michigan?" I asked.

"On everything," she said with a smile.

I was thinking about her plan on my walk home from school when Jake himself rode by on his bike. He stopped and said hello.

"So, do you live around here?" he asked me.

I pointed down the street. "Right there on the corner."

"Cool," he said. "So this is your kingdom."

I nodded, though I wasn't quite sure what he meant.

"Tell me about it," he said.

"Well, that's the Fredericksons' old house. They used to have a nasty pug dog. That's the spot where I wiped out on my bike ten years ago and got this scar." I pointed to a black spot on my elbow. "That's where Miss Tilden's house used to be. She was my favorite grown-up. Is that what you were looking for?" I asked, suddenly aware that I hadn't said anything very interesting at all.

"Yeah," he said, looking around. "What happened to Miss Tilden's house?"

I gazed up at the lot on the hill. "She went into a nursing home a few years ago, in another state. I don't even know if she's alive anymore. But they sold the place and the new buyer decided to take down the old house. I guess it should make me sad, but it actually looks prettier now. Miss Tilden didn't care about her house very much—it was small and kind of dingy. But she loved her wild yard and inviting all the animals in. So in a way, it's better now than ever."

"Until the new owners level the lot and put up their mansion, right?" Jake asked.

I stopped walking. "Do you think they'll do that?"

Jake shrugged. "They usually do." He walked me to my driveway and then got back on his bike. I felt elated and strangely disappointed at the same time. But before he left, I managed to invite him to go canoeing, and he agreed.

We paddled from Portage Lake to Delhi Park the following weekend. For much of that length, you feel like you're far away from everything that humans have made. Willows and weeds crowd the banks, and warblers chirp from the branches. A great blue heron led us for a mile down one stretch of the river, lifting up into the air with what seemed like irritated reluctance every time we rounded another bend. Painted turtles basked in the sun, clinging to fallen logs like oversized fungi.

Jake and I paddled in one canoe, while Delia paddled with our friend Michio in another.

"Is he suitably impressed?" Delia whispered to me when we stopped to have our lunch at a riverside park.

"I don't know," I told her

For most of the day, Jake and I talked about school and our families and our favorite bands. After lunch he told me more about Montana—about fly fishing with his father, about the Bitterroot Range that rose up south of Missoula, the moose and bears he'd spotted on hikes in the mountains.

We paddled under a highway overpass covered with graffiti. I wanted everything to be impressively beautiful, now more than ever, but it wasn't. Two dragonflies perched on a beer can floating near the water's edge. The water was greenish brown.

"Jake," I said quietly as we passed a family of mallards pecking on soggy bread slices that had been thrown in the water. "Does Montana really look like it did in *A River Runs through It?*"

"Yeah," he said. "Some places are that beautiful."

At the end of the day we sat at a picnic table in Delhi Park and waited for the canoe company to pick us up. True to form, Delia announced our plans for a frisbee game in the Arboretum the next week.

"That sounds fun," Jake said.

"You'll love the Arb," Delia said. "All the college students hang out there on the weekends. It's amazing."

Normally I would have chimed in, but this time I stayed silent. I wondered how our town arboretum would look to a person accustomed to ponderosa pines and snow-capped peaks. Crowded, probably. Humid and tame.

When the four of us parted ways, Jake thanked us for showing him the Huron River, but I thought he was just being polite. As soon as Delia and I were by ourselves, I told her I was through showing him the sights of Washtenaw County.

"But I thought you liked Jake," she said.

"I do, sort of," I told her. "But I'm sick of hearing about how great Montana is. He doesn't love it here the way you think he should, Delia. He's not impressed at all."

"Really?" she said. She rubbed a patch of river mud off her ankle. "Oh well, too bad. His loss."

"Right," I told her.

I wanted to be as unflappable as Delia, but I wasn't really. Every time I thought about Jake I felt annoyed. He had moved to my hometown without appreciating it the way I always had. But that was only part of it. What I really resented was that he'd made me notice its imperfections, too. Everywhere I looked now I noticed asphalt, overmanicured lawns, billboards, starlings. I'd never been as aware of so many consecutive cloudy days.

At school, I avoided Jake as much as I could. I figured that if I just stayed away long enough, I could shake off his influence and go back to only noticing the good things. I skipped the frisbee game with our friends the following weekend. When Jake asked me where I'd been, I just shrugged.

"Is something wrong, Liza?" he asked me.

"No," I said. "I guess I just thought it was going to rain."

The next Saturday, I woke to sunlight streaming through my window and the sound of people's voices coming from across the street. Two men and a woman were walking around Miss Tilden's lot. Arms folded across their chests, they were looking at the yard in a way that seemed territorial. It made me uneasy.

"Who are those people across the street?" I asked my mother. She got up from the breakfast table and went to the window.

"Those are the Franklins," she said. "They're the ones who bought the lot, remember? Jessie Calhoun says they've found an architect and are busy making their plans."

"So they're really going to build?" I asked.

"A big one, apparently," she said, going back to her seat.

"Will they get rid of the forsythia bushes? The pine trees?" I asked. "Miss Tilden would hate that."

"I don't know what they're going to do, Liza," my mother said. "But it's their place now. Are you going to have something to eat?"

I didn't want breakfast. Overwhelmed by too many feelings, I set out for a long run. I ran down through the Arboretum, along the railroad tracks beside the Huron River, then back up through my neighborhood, crisscrossing as many streets as I could. The maples were at their peak, orange and red exclamations at the streets' edges. When a strong breeze blew, a flurry of leaves would fall from the trees and settle across the grass.

I ran along the edge of the curb, angrily kicking up piles of red maple leaves, tawny oaks, yellow redbuds.

I kicked for the new owners of Miss Tilden's lot, who didn't respect the things she had loved.

I kicked for Jake Peterson, who was right about all the wrong things.

I kicked the leaves high into the air. They made a dry shuffling sound with my every kick, a sound that had always been one of my favorites of the fall. Maybe that's why I eventually stopped kicking. I ran on, leaves and leaf fragments clinging to my shoelaces.

I crossed Stadium and ran through Park Washtenaw, up and down the meadow trails. By the time I turned back toward home, my frustration had dissipated. Perhaps it was the effects of the long run. Or maybe it was just the brilliance of the autumn day, winning me over.

When I reached my block, I walked up the driveway of Miss Tilden's lot and sat on the hilltop grass. A pair of fat fox squirrels chased each other up and down a trunk, and a breeze rustled the pine trees behind me. Looking down the hill at my yard, I could see the places where Delia and I had once played—the blue spruce, the pear tree, the scratchy junipers. Everything looked familiar, but small—like I could reach out and cup it all in my hands.

This was my kingdom—Jake had said it himself. A kingdom of robins and grass and mallards and murky rivers. It was a place of gentle relief, and skies that were gray as often as blue. It was not, I knew, the sort of dazzling world a person would fall in love with in a day. But maybe that was better. Maybe that made this unastonishing place all the more mine.

A bicycle whizzed down the street in front of me and turned up my driveway. It was Jake. He wouldn't know where to find me, and at first I thought I'd just let him leave. But when I saw him walking his bike down the driveway, I stood up, brushed off my running shorts, and shouted down the hill.

"Hey!" I called.

He looked up and waved, then walked up to join me.

"What are you doing up here—communing with Miss Tilden's spirit?" he asked me.

"Sort of," I said.

We sat down on the grass.

"You know," I told him, "you were right. The owners are going to put up a giant house here. Soon."

Jake nodded, but I couldn't tell how much he cared.

"I guess that doesn't sound tragic to you," I said wryly. "It's not bear country or anything."

Jake watched a mourning dove settle on the telephone wire in front of the lot. "Liza, I miss my home," he said. "But that doesn't mean there's anything wrong with yours."

"I know," I told him. For a moment I was silent, thinking of so many things I could say. In the end I said almost nothing. "I finally figured that out."

Across the street, the new owner of the Fredericksons' house started up his noisy leaf blower. He had already filled up six large bags and by the time he had cleared every leaf scrap off his lawn he would probably fill six more. I hated his mechanical tidying of my kingdom and I had half a mind to come back that night and shake out all the bags on Miss Tilden's hilltop, to release the leaves into the cold air and let them dry and rot in their messy, essential way. But for the moment I had other plans.

"This would be a great day for apple picking," I told Jake.

He smiled. "Count me in."

A native of Ann Arbor, **Sara St. Antoine** *now lives in Cambridge, Massachusetts. She returns to Michigan often to visit some of her favorite people and places.*

Reapers and Sowers

Christmas Tree Miracle

CAROL FARLEY

Among the most important natural resources of northern Minnesota, Wisconsin, Michigan, and New York are their forests of spruce and pine. The region's original white pine forests, felled more than a century ago to make timber masts and other wood products, are mostly gone now. But the forests that have grown in their place continue to provide a steady source of timber and, of course, Christmas trees.

Sailors know that sailing the Great Lakes can be even more dangerous than navigating the oceans because storms can strike so quickly. The winter months can be especially treacherous when blizzards of tremendous power suddenly spring up and rage across the water. Lake Michigan, with almost 350 unbroken miles of water, is known as the most tempestuous.

In 1912, Hermann Schuenemann recognized the dangers, but he had an early-winter mission to perform. As captain of the schooner *Rouse Simmons,* he would sail from Michigan's Upper Peninsula every holiday season to bring fresh Christmas trees to the people of Chicago. For twelve years, in early November, he and his crew had loaded trees from Thompson, a small village near Manisteque, and sailed down Lake Michigan off the coast of Wisconsin. When they docked in Chicago's harbor, they would be greeted by eager customers glad to pay a dollar for a Michigan Christmas tree.

Preparations in November of 1912 began as usual. Soon trees were piled so high on the deck of the *Rouse Simmons* that bystanders on shore said the ship looked like a floating pine forest. On November 23, Captain Hermann and his crew of sixteen set out. There were reports of bad weather ahead, but the captain felt he had to deliver his holiday cargo on time. His brother, August Schuenemann, had perished in a shipwreck years before, so Captain Hermann respected the power of Great Lake storms. But he was certain that the *Rouse Simmons* would get through.

Nobody knows exactly what befell the ship and her crew as a horrendous gale-blizzard with snow, hail, and strong winds raged across Lake Michigan during the next few days. Most ships never left their ports. On November 28, a Wisconsin Life Saving Station in Kewaunee reported seeing a three-masted schooner similar to the *Rouse Simmons* lying low in the water, distress flags flying. But they were unable to fight through the storm to provide assistance or even to positively identify it.

The Christmas tree ship never reached its harbor. Suspicion that it sank with all hands aboard became a certainty as evidence washed ashore. A note from the first mate was found floating in a bottle. "Schooner R. S. ready to go down" was part of the message. Many years later, Captain Hermann's wallet was pulled in by a fisherman, its contents waterlogged but still readable.

In 1912, however—in the very same month the ship disappeared—the most compelling proof that the ship had gone down was the floating cargo. Christmas trees soon began drifting ashore, and they inspired a small miracle. Volunteers hauled them to the regular Clark Street market, where a brave woman waited. Barbara Schuenemann, the skipper's widow, conducted business as usual. Despite the tragedy of the lost ship and the death of seventeen men, the Christmas trees were offered for sale, just as they had been offered in past years. As usual, Captain Hermann's holiday cargo was there to brighten the holidays for hundreds of people.

Mrs. Schuenemann continued to sell Christmas trees at the Clark Street wharf every December for the next twenty-two years. Most people today have forgotten her, but the story of the miracle trees of 1912 and the men from the *Rouse Simmons* who delivered them is still vividly remembered.

❧

Carol Farley *has written numerous books and stories for young people. Many of these tales take place in Michigan, where she was born. Others are set in Korea, where she lived for several years.*

Journal Entry:
Lake Michigan, July

ROGER PFINGSTON

Writing, how quiet
I am. Chipmunk and sparrow
Visit my small porch.

A retired teacher of English and photography, **Roger Pfingston**
now devotes much of his time to writing poetry and making photo-
graphs. He is the recipient of a poetry fellowship from the National
Endowment for the Arts and a Teacher Creativity Fellowship for pho-
tography from the Lilly Endowment.

Summer at
Silver Creek Farm

Shannon Sexton

Silver Creek Farm, located in rural Hiram, Ohio, produces certified or-ganic poultry, vegetables, fruits, and herbs. This story takes place during the unusually wet summer of 2000, and is told by Jamie, a fourteen-year-old fulfilling her eighth grade service project hours, eager to record the ad-ventures she has along the way.

May 16

Mom and I have a garden at home—a little patch of land that's nice and manicured. Neat rows, no weeds, and you always pick up your tools when the day is over. How different from this farm, a place in progress.

If you flew in an airplane low over the fields, you would see hawks circling above the woods, searching for food; moun-tains of compost destined to blanket the fields; rows covered with cloth rolled out like giant toilet paper to protect the broc-coli, squash, and lettuce; a pond, two barns, a half-constructed pavilion, and a farmhouse; tractors abandoned mid-row; tiny dots of sheep milling around in the pasture; and Silver Creek, which runs along a boundary of the farm.

Molly and Ted Bartlett run a program called CSA, which stands for Community Supported Agriculture. About a hun-dred people become members of the farm during the growing season. The CSAers receive a weekly share of produce and an invitation to explore the farm all summer long.

Ted, a retired professor, reminds me of Santa Claus in his suspenders, jolly with a twinkle in his eyes. Molly is a potter. She has a young but sun-worn face and braided hair, and she likes to give advice.

The two of them have run this farm since 1985, and it's been certified organic since 1988. In the state of Ohio, Ted told me, "certified organic" means food grown on land that has been chemical-free for at least three years, so first they had to nurse the soil back to health.

The Bartletts introduced me to the workers today. Eric, a nature lover in his forties, has worked here for years. Rebecca is a tall, quiet woman so at home in the fields that I can't imagine her anywhere else. Shannon and Jen, two summer interns from Hiram College, are new to full-time farming. Meghan is the closest to my age, a seventeen-year-old who just graduated from Burton High. She volunteered here in the fall and liked it so much she wanted this to be her summer job. Last but not least is Rachel, a science teacher who grew up on a farm and just started working here full time.

May 19

Baby chicks arrived by airmail today! I couldn't believe it—120 four-ounce chicks, shipped in a flat box with air holes and postage stamps. Yellow blobs of wiggle and fuzz were packed into compartments before they were a day old.

"Puffballs," Rebecca remarked as I squatted in their pen, which was carpeted with cedar shavings. When you pick up a puffball, it makes a slow, protesting chirp, its legs twirling like windmills in your hand. Eric taught me how to dip their beaks in water and food. This was the chicks' first meal, and since they have no mother, we had to show them what to do. After eating, they scurried off to huddle under the heat lamps, like campers crowding around a fire.

May 20

Planting onions, squatting, sinking. The slurp and suction of the mud. Sprays of rain. Molly says all the crops are going in late this year because of it.

May 23

If only Mom knew, I am volunteering to play in the mud. Already I can't get the dirt out of my fingernails. And why bother? Jen and Shannon say it's pointless to shower at the end of the day sometimes—they'll just get mud-caked again tomorrow, and they're too tired.

May 24

I remember Ted yelling to Molly over the roar of the tractor today. "Jamie looks like she's getting sunburnt, doesn't she?" He drives toward me. Everyone is planting potatoes. "Skin cancer in this area is on the rise," he warns me as the tractor plods on by.

"I put sunscreen on," I say sheepishly. It's one of the few times I've spoken out loud.

May 26

Funny that among nuts and bolts, electric drills, and screwdrivers, an egg rumbled from the inside out and burst open with a tiny life. Ted told us that several chicks hatched on his workbench today. He found one dead in the doorway, and another one shuddering nearby. I made the survivor a home in a cardboard box, since it was too small to go in with the older chicks. Later, Eric found a third one and we put it in there, too.

While the airmailed chicks are raised for meat and kept in coops, the other chickens are egg layers. They are free to roam the farm during daylight hours. At night, Molly shoos them back into their coops where they're safe from raccoons, hawks, and foxes. Sometimes a few sneak off and nest elsewhere. That's why we get surprises like the workbench chicks.

June 1

Dreary day but refreshingly cool. All the chickens have parasites now, though, because it's been so wet. Their coops are muddy and stink like urine and lime. We had to put Ren-o-sol pills in their water, bubbles slowly rising as the pills dissolved, turning the water green—like an Alka Seltzer commercial.

June 4

Weeding carrots, weeding carrots, weeding carrots. Meghan, her pigtails peeping out from under her sunhat, saying, "This is, like, torture." Sun beating on our backs. Going nowhere. Miles and miles of green.

June 7

We spent the morning barefoot, ankle deep in the mud, covering long rows of beans that wriggled their way up to the surface, like earthworms gasping for air after a storm. Mud curled like ribbons between my toes, cool as the water in a creek, and as comforting.

The summer of 2000—summer of the rains. This isn't the Ohio we're used to. We're used to drought, the grass scorched dishwater blond. Not this eternal mud, sucking, slurping, sinking.

Ted says all the irrigation lines the workers walked across the field are useless. Molly says, do a sun dance. Pray for sun. "We're more equipped to deal with a drought than the rains."

June 8

Now I know how a woman's back must hurt when she's pregnant. I've been carrying a bucket of blueberries around my waist all morning. And my feet hurt, too! It's boring, alone in the bushes for hours with no one to talk to but the starlings and sparrows that are stealing the berries, even under the netting, before I can reach them. A CSAer passes by and I ask him what time it is, and groan. So, so hungry. Just the sound of blueberries drumming the plastic bucket, like a bunch of ten-cent rubber balls.

June 10

We did the most disgusting thing today—squashing larvae! It was my fault, too. I was the first one out to the field, and I noticed that a couple of plants were speckled with orange larvae and had holes in their leaves. I asked Rebecca what they were. Boy, was I sorry I asked. They're the larvae of the Colorado potato beetle. How they got all the way to Ohio, don't ask me.

What you have to do is pull each side of the leaf together and pop them between your fingers. They squirt big bubbles of juice, and stain your fingers orange. The boys in my school would love that.

I admit, I swallowed a squeal when Rebecca showed me what to do, like it was the most normal thing in the world. Ted said it's better than spraying pesticides on the plants, though, and if we let the larvae grow into beetles, they'll destroy the whole crop.

June 11

Well, at least there's one good thing about this rain. The farm is bursting with blueberries and peas. The problem is, the animals are hungry, too. Deer keep trampling through the pea plants, eating and destroying the crop.

Molly, who is full of ideas, thought of a solution. After gathering forty old eggs from the barns, she scattered them along the rows of peas. Rotten eggs let off a sulfuric gas that she hopes will keep the deer away.

June 14

All morning, harvesting carrots—the CSAers, full-time workers, Molly, Ted, and me. Everyone jumping on pitchforks, driving them into the ground, the sound of roots groaning and snapping, dirt shifting, the ground erupting in orange.

These aren't the kind of carrots you see at Giant Eagle—they're half the size, and they all look different, like corkscrews, witches' gnarly fingers, or the braids in Meghan's hair. Some are split down the sides, like they laughed too hard.

Mrs. Wilson says she rejoined the CSA this year just for the carrots. One hundred percent crunch, and super sweet, fresh out of the ground. No grocery store compares. Andy, her toddler, called a pair that were stuck together "kissing carrots," and begged to take them home.

June 15

Hens pick the most interesting places to lay their eggs. Today, chicks hatched in a nest shaded by the gas tank—the word DIESEL spelled in red, on a white label, the silver cylinder on its side. I saw the darling peeps, seconds old, and counted—eleven yellow, one black. They were soooo cute! To think, before I volunteered here, I'd never seen a peep, and now I've seen hundreds in just a couple of weeks!

June 17

Eleven of the chicks died last night from hypothermia. I wanted to cry when Shannon told me. She and Jen said it rained last night and then the temperature dropped (they should know, they live in a tent), and the tiny peeps couldn't stay warm. Rachel found the dead ones huddled together, another sign that they died of hypothermia. I can't believe so many died. Even though they were alive for less than a day, something's missing now that they're gone. The remaining chick, trailing behind its mother, seems so lost and alone.

June 18

Another crazy bug day, this time in the green beans. Holes through all the leaves, yellow cotyledons, plants tipping over at the stem, like snapped or broken twigs that are still attached. And bugs all over the place.

Because the weather is chilly and wet, Molly said, the plants are stressed and vulnerable to insects. Mexican bean beetles are taking advantage of this. Some look like bronze ladybugs, while others are more oblong, scarlet red, and faster at flying.

We had to pick off the beetles and put them in Ziploc bags. How absurd! Hundreds of beetles zigzagging along the plastic. Then moving slower and slower because they couldn't breathe.

I'm not very fond of bugs, but I felt bad about them suffocating. I'd never really killed anything until I volunteered here. Molly says it's just the cycle of life. Bugs, plants, animals, humans—everything struggles to survive. For this farm to survive, some bugs have to be killed.

But lots of bugs are helpful to the farm. Ladybugs, praying mantises, ants, and bees all help the crops. The hornets in the blueberry bushes, for example, are pollinators. Without insects like them, we wouldn't have blueberries! I just wish the pollinators didn't sting.

June 21

Picked garlic scapes, elegant as swan necks. Harvested sugar peas. Weeded carrots. In the middle of a row, a garter snake slalomed its way across my path, thin and brown with a yellow stripe on its back. I was glad I wasn't barefoot.

June 25

How does Molly always know when it's going to rain? Today we were composting onions, feet and hands caked in mud, when the radio crackled and whooshed.

"Okay, everybody," Molly said in her slow drawl, "looks like it's going to rain. How about heading for the tent till it blows over?"

We looked at the still, gray sky and disagreed, continuing our work. But a minute later everything darkened, the trees rustled, and the wind began to blow. We looked at each other and the sky, and ran toward the tent, but we got caught in sheets of rain.

June 27

There are a million words for things here that I don't know. Ten thousand kinds of tools and tomatoes and lettuces. Maybe I will grow up to be a scientist, or even a farmer. All I know is that I have so much to learn.

June 28

"Don't mess up the mud!" Molly joked this morning. We were barefoot again, hoeing soggy rows of green beans. Molly left us there and wandered over to the peas to check their production. Boy, was everyone surprised when she came back! Molly found an arrowhead between two rows of peas. This was after a rainstorm, and she was looking for *anything* but an arrowhead. It almost looked like some kind of symbol, sitting there on the surface of the mud.

Funny to think of a Native American sinking in this very mud, centuries ago, just like we were today. Last year in history class, Mr. Hillary said that the Hopewell were an early tribe in this area, and later the Shawnee, Iroquois, and Erie came. I wonder who designed this arrowhead? I think of all the struggles and hardships of this land over the years.

I've heard murmurs among the workers doubting that the

farm will produce enough crops to feed the CSAers. Sometimes Molly snaps at people and doesn't mean to, but you can tell she's stressed. Even Ted seems to struggle, tinkering with broken machinery in the tractor barn, away from people, on the days when it's hard to see the twinkle in his eye.

The arrowhead was just lying there, plain as day. I think it was a sign of hope. The Bartletts have been farming here for fifteen years, and they have always made it. I think that they will continue to survive.

Shannon Sexton *played in the dirt at Silver Creek Farm during the years she spent attending Hiram College. The details in this story are true. Sexton currently lives in eastern Pennsylvania and serves as the managing editor of* Yoga International.

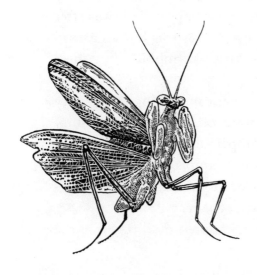

Weekend

ROBERT ALEXANDER

All weekend long it rained and the wind blew leaves and walnuts out of the tree in Ralph's backyard. There was occasional lightning and Ralph heard the booming of walnuts on the roof as rather benign artillery, though he wouldn't want one to hit him on the head.

On Monday the rain had stopped and Ralph woke to the sound of geese squawking up beneath the still-solid clouds. The walnuts were mostly gone from the tree (for another two years), the leaves also, the bare branches looking already in mid-September like they would in the middle of winter. Walnuts lay across the lawn like small green baseballs . . . over a hundred, Ralph figured, on his small patch of backyard. All day long Ralph looks out his window to see the squirrel so flushed with food he's doing acrobatics on the hammock. He leaps from the tree, runs, stops, jumps up to the hammock, holds on for a few seconds, then flips in the air, once, twice, again . . . and jumps back to the tree.

At dusk, when light is barely light, one of Ralph's cardinals comes to feed at the feeder just beyond his window. Ralph has come to think of the birds as his, he supposes it's the same pair he sees, always this time of year by themselves. In the spring Ralph noticed how, holding a single seed in their beaks, they would give each other sunflower seeds. But now they come alone, and the quiet sounds Ralph hears like squeaks while they peck at the sunflower seeds are, he would like to imagine, for him.

Robert Alexander *is a graduate of the creative writing program at the University of Wisconsin–Milwaukee. He edits the Marie Alexander Poetry Series (White Pine Press), and has written a Civil War narrative,* Five Forks: Waterloo of the Confederacy *(Michigan State University Press, 2003). He divides his time between Shorewood Hills, Wisconsin (on Lake Mendota), and Grand Marais, Michigan (on Lake Superior).*

Serious Fishing

JOHN KNOTT

Everywhere in the Great Lakes, from small towns to big cities, one can find dedicated fishermen who slip away from the bustling streets to enjoy the rhythms and harvests of a fish-filled river.

Charles Morris has been fishing the Huron River for fifty-five years, since he was six. He can tell you about every good hole and fishing place from Barton Pond to Belleville Lake, with the kind of affectionate detail that suggests long and intimate experience. He can tell you about the ones that have changed or disappeared, too, like the sandbar that's harder to get to now because of a wall along the bank, or the large pond that was filled in when the Ypsilanti Ford plant expanded, or the marshes that used to be where the parking lot for the plant is now. He remembers how the big kids used to club spawning carp in the spring in those marshes. If you wonder about eating carp, he'll tell you that it's as good-tasting a fish as you can get out of the river, that it seasons well, and that when it's smoked it can be mistaken for smoked coho salmon.

Huron River Carp

Fillet the fish and take the mud vein out. Use seasoned pepper and garlic pepper. Squeeze a lemon over the slabs. Slice the peel up and put it around the sides. Bake the same way you would salmon.

Morris doesn't plan fishing trips: "If you've got the time, you take off." He might try a favorite hole at 8:30 some summer evening and come back with an eighteen-inch walleye and a sixteen-inch channel catfish caught in the same spot, using the same lure, as he did on one recent outing. Since he has always lived within walking distance of the river (in Ypsilanti) and keeps a couple of rods "loaded," spur-of-the-moment fishing is no problem. He uses waders, and sometimes a canoe, to get into places he couldn't otherwise and sneak up on a few bass. He fishes a lot in his fourteen-foot wood and canvas rowboat, now sixty years old, and has a bigger boat that he can use to fish the Detroit River with his father-in-law. Morris likes fishing the cuts that go back into the marshes on Walpole Island and will spend several days with friends catching and cleaning fish there, but he finds all the fish he can eat in the Huron: "You can catch everything you want just below Peninsula Dam." Sometimes fishing the Huron is "almost too easy," he says.

Morris knows the fishing scene up and down the river around Ann Arbor and Ypsilanti and can tell you what you can expect to find at just about any time and place, not only the fish but the people. Fishing for crappie off Barton Dam in the spring, he says, you practically have to make reservations. If you leave your spot for a minute, you lose it. Every fall along the river he sees some of the same regulars who come out from

East Detroit or Lincoln Park or Livonia to fish for walleye in Ann Arbor. If there are too many people trying to fish the same ledge, they just cast in rotation. They get along because they know how to fish, according to Morris. He now sees kids fishing the same holes he did when he was their age. Sometimes older "kids," in their twenties and thirties, watch him fish a hole to see if the fish are biting. They call him "the jig man," because he likes to fish with jigs. He will fish in the winter near the dams, where the river doesn't freeze, and has caught walleye on Christmas Eve and given them to friends for Christmas dinner.

Walleye

Cook walleye any way you want. To fry, put fillets in a bowl with Drake's batter mix, add seasoning, and pour in some good Canadian beer. The best way to eat it is to start with the "cheeks and chins." The cheeks are the round pieces behind the eyes; the chin is the triangular piece behind the gill plate (where the fish's chin would be if it had one).

Morris knows what to do with the various kinds of fish he catches in the river, including Northern pike, a notoriously bony fish that he claims to be able to debone. He tells a story about the time a friend suggested a fish fry, and he said, "Give me two hours." He went to his favorite sandbar and caught four carp on dough balls in the first half hour, then spent the next hour and a half cutting them up and cooking them, for four couples. He and his friends and family obviously know how to eat well, and they enjoy some dishes many of us would not recognize as part of the local cuisine, like turtle gumbo, made with snapping turtle meat.

Turtle Gumbo

Always use snapping turtle. Chop up bell pepper, green onion (maybe yellow), and garlic. Add tomato sauce and a couple of bay leaves. Add okra (or corn cut in two-inch rounds), canned tomatoes and a couple of fresh ones. You can season the meat and batter fry it just enough to seal it, then add it to the pot. Cook it until the meat starts falling off the bone.

According to Morris, a friend from Louisiana makes spaghetti sauce with turtle meat, so hot that you can hardly eat it and so good that you can't stop.

Fishing is so natural and habitual for Charles Morris that he talks about it easily, with a ready supply of metaphors. He describes fishing the holes along the Huron as like going shopping. If you don't find what you want at one store, you just go on to the next one. He tells friends that he shows where to fish: "I took you to the market. You do your own shopping." Years of watching people fish have made him a shrewd judge of human nature. He talks about three kinds of fishermen: people who go out and hope something will come by, people who know something ought to come by, and people who don't care whether something comes by or not. They just want to get out of the house. You can usually find Charles Morris at the front desk of the Ann Arbor Public Library, bantering with patrons while he checks out their books. If you ask him about the river, you'll get some stories.

John Knott *is a professor of English at the University of Michigan. He is the author of several books, including* Imagining Wild America, *and an editor of the anthology* The Huron River: Voices from the Watershed.

The Worm Girl

LAURA LUSH

I am the Worm Girl.
I drive a Wonder Bread truck,
converted—good tires,
bumpers black as jujubes.
Every weekend I drive the Grey Bruce County,
all the silvered lakes,
birches waving like old drunks.
In back I have 25,000 worms
deep in earth
like coins in a chocolate cake.
Sometimes they wriggle to the top,
luminous as half-moons,
their skins onion-blue.
What they feel is my hand,
each finger a lure
urging them gently out
like a carrot's midwife.
I reward them with light.

Laura Lush *was born in Brantford, Ontario. She is the author of several books of poetry, and publishes regularly in literary magazines in Canada and abroad.*

Neengay, the Story Giver

DAY ALEXANDER

In 1855, Henry Wadsworth Longfellow wrote The Song of Hiawatha *about a legendary hero, Hiawatha, who lived on the shores of Lake Superior. "Whence came these stories?" Longfellow asked in the book's prologue. He never knew that many of them came from a young Ojibwe girl who lived in what is now northern Wisconsin.*

Neengay, Woman of the Forest Meadow, was born at Chequamegon Bay on southwestern Lake Superior in the year 1777. She was the eldest daughter of Waubojeeg, chief of the Ojibwe village that lay on a shaftlike point of land jutting into the bay. Her father was a great war chief, leading his warriors in a battle at St. Croix Falls in 1783 against the Foxes and the Dakotas. After the battle, the Dakotas moved westward and the Foxes retreated to the south.

The land that surrounded Chequamegon Bay was thick with forests of cedar, pine, hemlock, and birch. Red sandstone, layered like plates, edged the icy waters of Lake Superior. The lake, scooped out by glaciers during the last Ice Age, was so vast it made its own weather.

Neengay and her family bent their lives to the seasons, as trees bend in the wind. They hunted animals in the forests, caught fish in the cold waters, gathered wild rice, harvested maple sugar, and picked ripe berries, always preparing for the coming winter.

As Neengay grew from child to young woman, she listened to the stories her father told: tales of great deeds, tales of cold winters, of death, of love, and tales about a hero named Wenibojo (whom Longfellow renamed Hiawatha). The land formed the stories just as the glaciers had shaped the lake.

Winter dominated their lives, lasting for six months. The stories reflected their concern for food during those cold times when the wind swept off the iced-over lake.

When the north wind brewed up a storm in late winter, it was named Papuckewis, both a wind and the hero of this story.

Papuckewis and the North Wind

In old times, during a long winter, Papuckewis and his family had very little food. Though he tried to catch fish in the lake, no fish would take his hook. The caribou, the deer, the beaver had also disappeared from his hunting grounds. Papuckewis did not know what to do.

One day he was hunting along the icebound shores of the lake where the winds had piled up the ice into strange shapes that to Papuckewis looked like dwellings.

"Surely," he said to himself, "the north wind, Kiwedin, lives in one of these ice dwellings. I will ask him for help."

With great ceremony, Papuckewis smoked his pipe and offered Kiwedin some tobacco. Kiwedin heard his prayer and told him to fill his sacks with ice and snow and then return home. When he came to the hill near his wigwam, Papuckewis was to leave the sacks until morning. At dawn he would find them filled with fish.

"This I will do!" Papuckewis said.

"I give you one warning," Kiwedin roared. "Do not look

back at your sacks even though you may hear voices shouting, 'Thief! Thief!'"

Everything went as Kiwedin had told Papuckewis. He filled his sacks with ice and snow and left them on the hill near his wigwam. As he walked away, Papuckewis heard voices crying, "Thief! Thief!" but he did not turn around.

The next day Wenibojo came to visit him. Papuckewis had brought back his sacks filled with fish, so he and his family were having a feast. Papuckewis offered some fish to Wenibojo.

"Where did you find all this fish?" Wenibojo asked. He wished to get food without working for it.

Papuckewis told him how he had prayed to Kiwedin, who directed him to fill his sacks with ice and snow and to leave them near his own wigwam.

"I will go and do the same," cried Wenibojo, jumping up and down with excitement.

"But," warned Papuckewis, "on no account must you turn and look behind you, even though you hear voices calling you."

Wenibojo raced to the ice dwellings and prayed to Kiwedin. As he was in a great hurry, he rushed the ceremony with the tobacco. He filled up many sacks with ice and snow and hurried back to a hill near his own wigwam.

As he was running to his wigwam, he heard voices behind him, crying, "Thief! Thief! Wenibojo has stolen fish from Kiwedin. Catch him! Muckumick! Muckumick!"

The voices were so loud that Wenibojo turned his head to see who was there. Behind him the north wind blew. The next morning when Wenibojo opened his sacks, he found only ice and snow.

As a punishment for Wenibojo's greediness, Kiwedin ordered him to run over the hills with his bags of ice and snow during the Moon of Crusted Snow. This storm is called

Papuckewis. And so Wenibojo runs with the north wind crying behind him, "Thief! Thief! Stop him! Muckumick! Muckumick!"

Neengay and the family followed the moons that the Ojibwe named for what happened in nature. They lived at the long wigwam on Chequamegon Bay during Flower Moon, Strawberry Moon, Raspberry Moon, Wild Rice Moon, and Shining Leaf Moon. Then they traveled to their own hunting grounds when Moon of Falling Leaves was in the sky. In that lonely place they hunted the beaver and other animals during Freezing Moon, Little Spirit Moon, Great Spirit Moon, Moon of the Eagle, and Moon of Crusted Snow. After catching the maple sugar in Sap Running Moon, the family returned to the great wigwam on Chequamegon Bay.

In this way, Neengay lived until her fifteenth year. But in 1791, change came to her life when John Johnston, a young Ulster Irish fur trader, arrived at the Ojibwe village.

Johnston set up a fur trading post nearby. During that year, he fell in love with Neengay and asked Waubojeeg's permission to marry her.

His answer to the young man has come down to us.

"Johnston, your customs are not our customs. You white men desire our women. You marry them, and when they cease to please your eye, you say they are not your wives and you forsake them. Return to Montreal, young friend, with your load of skins. And if there the women of the pale faces do not put my daughter out of your mind, come back here and we will talk again. She is young and can wait."

Fasting was a way to seek guidance in the Ojibwe life, especially for young men and women who searched for guardian spirits. Deep in the forest behind the village, Neengay fasted to reach a decision. On the fourth day of her fast she returned to her family, laying cedar boughs along the path to the wigwam. She told of her fasting dream, and this, too, was recorded.

"I painted my face black with soot from the fire and began my fast in silence and alone. I dreamed two times of a white man whose face I could not see. He presented gifts to all of us.

"The white man had a tin cup and he gave me a drink of water. By his side was a dog who looked up to my face as if he knew me.

"On the last day of my fast, I dreamed again. I saw the man's face and it was the face of John Johnston."

Months later, Johnston returned to the Ojibwe village, still in love with Neengay, who accepted him to be her husband. They were married, and in 1793 traveled by canoe with an infant son, Lewis Saurin, to St. Mary's, now named Sault Ste. Marie, 350 miles away on the eastern edge of Lake Superior. John Johnston built a fine home on the banks of the St. Mary's River, where he established a fur trading business.

No longer would Neengay follow the paths of the Ojibwe moons.

Seven more children were born to her. By the kitchen fire, Neengay told the stories to her children using the Ojibwe words. Though she understood the English language, she never spoke it.

So the years passed. The children grew up. In 1814, the area became part of the United States.

In 1822, Henry Rowe Schoolcraft, a newly appointed agent for Indian affairs, came to the town. He lodged with the Johnston family. A year later he married Jane, the oldest daughter.

Schoolcraft became interested in the stories that the Johnston children had heard from Neengay. "Who would have thought that such stories could come from these woodland people, who are not acquainted with the world," he wrote. During the winter of 1826, he asked them to translate some of the stories.

Neengay said to her children, "I only wish that I could tell the stories as my father told them to me and not rely on my relatives."

Schoolcraft sent handwritten issues of *The Literary Voyageur,* containing the stories, to his friends. In 1839 he published these stories and others in *Algic Researches.* Longfellow read that book and used the stories in it.

Neengay never received recognition for the stories, though they were a part of her, of her father Waubojeeg, and of her children.

John Johnston died in 1828. After his death his wife returned more to the ways of the Ojibwe. By an Indian Treaty she was given some land on Sugar Island near the town. Each spring she harvested the maple sugar from the trees.

Neengay died in 1843. She was sixty-six years old. Her children said that the following story was her favorite.

Sigwan and Bibon—Spring and Winter

An old man from the north, gray haired and leaning on a staff, went roaming over the countryside. Looking around him one day, after traveling for five moons, he found a place to rest himself.

He was seated a short time when he saw before him a young man, very handsome, with red cheeks and sparkling eyes. His hair was covered with flowers, and from his lips he blew a breath that was as sweet as the wild rose.

The old man leaned forward on his staff and said to the young man, "Rest here with me and we will talk a little. But first, let us build up a fire."

They made the fire and the two took their seats beside it. Presently, the young man felt cold. He looked about to see what could have caused this terrible coldness and he pressed his hands against his cheeks to keep them warm.

The old man bragged. "When I wish to cross a river, I breathe upon it and I make it hard. Then I walk upon its surface. The tread of my foot makes soft things hard. Oh, my power is never ending."

The young man, feeling colder every moment, began to speak as the sun burst onto the land. "I, too, go over all the earth. I have seen it covered with snow, and the waters hard as stone. But when I pass over them, the snow melts, the streams begin to flow, the rivers move, the ice melts upon the lakes. The earth becomes green beneath my steps, the flowers blossom, the birds are joyful, and all the power of which you speak vanishes!"

The old man drew a deep breath and said, "I know who you are! You are Sigwan! You are Spring!"

"True," replied the young man. "Look at my head. Do you not see that it is crowned with flowers and that my cheeks are rosy? You are Bibon! You are Winter! I know that your power is great, but, old man, now you do not dare to come to this country for your strength will fail!"

Bibon felt this truth and when the morning sun came in all its warm shining, he spoke once more to Sigwan. "Sigwan, I will return to this country in many moons, and then it will be I who will be the victor."

With that, Bibon vanished away.

As a child, **Day Alexander** *visited her grandparents on Lake Superior's Chequamegon Bay and she now returns each year. A storyteller and a former Washington, D.C., school librarian, she lives in Boulder, Colorado. She is writing a novel about Neengay,* The Story Keeper, *which includes more Ojibwe stories. Her published works include* The Legend of the Treaty Oak, A Forgotten Tale of Washington, D.C., The Gift to the Selkie, *and* Jump, Clap, and Sing: Singing Games of Washington, D.C., Children.

Apple Jelly

MARGARET ATWOOD

No sense in all this picking,
peeling & simmering
if sheer food is all
you want; you can buy it cheaper.

Why then do we burn our hours
& muscles in this stove,
cut our thumbs, to get these tiny
glass pots of clear jelly?

Hoarded in winter: the sun
on that noon, your awkward leap
down from the tree,
licked fingers, sweet pink juice,
what we keep
the taste of the act, taste
of this day.

Margaret Atwood *is the author of numerous collections of poetry and such novels as* The Handmaid's Tale, Cat's Eye, *and* Alias Grace. *She lives in Ontario.*

The Box Camera

EDWIN WAY TEALE

Edwin Way Teale spent his boyhood summers on his grandparents' farm in northern Indiana. In addition to helping out with farm work, he ventured for hours every day into the surrounding forests, swamps, and dunes, developing outdoor knowledge and skills that he would use for the rest of his life.

In the shade of the old oak tree, I scribbled down figures on the wooden top of a strawberry crate. A Sears, Roebuck catalogue lay in the grass beside me. I was busy figuring up exactly how many strawberries I would have to pick in order to obtain an object of my heart's desire.

Oftentimes, as I walked about the fields of Lone Oak or lay in the meadow-grass looking up at the drifting clouds or stole noiselessly along the mossy trails of the north woods, I had wished that I could record pictures of all the things I saw. Now I had decided to make this wish come true.

A few years before, when I was about eight years old, an uncle of mine had given me an oddity camera which had been produced at the time of the World's Columbian Exposition at Chicago, in 1893. It was the size and shape of a watch and had been designed to make miniature pictures, half as big as a postage stamp. Although no film was made to fit the camera, and its mechanism was then out of order, I used to carry it about with me, snapping imaginary pictures of birds' nests and wind-blown trees and long V's of autumn geese.

This summer, however, my heart was set on a real camera.

In the Sears, Roebuck catalogue I found listed a complete outfit—a box camera, a roll of film, a developing kit and printing material—all for $3.75. At that time of year the quickest source of money was the strawberry patch. Gramp paid me a cent and a half a quart for picking the berries. My figures on the white wood of the crate-top revealed that I would have to pick 250 quarts to obtain the needed sum.

The berries ran about eighty to the quart. That made a grand total of 20,000 strawberries which stood between me and the realization of my desire. I could visualize myself stooping over and picking off a berry and putting it in a box once, twice, three times, ten times, a hundred times, a thousand times, twenty thousand times!

Nevertheless, I set to work. I asked Gramp to keep all my tally slips until I had the whole 250 quarts. Each evening I would ask him how the score stood. Progress was always disappointing, but the total mounted day by day. Finally the 250 quarts were picked and the money was mine. I made out the order carefully and printed the address on an envelope. Gramp came by while I was thus engaged. He volunteered:

"Better write large. Th' man may be deaf."

As soon as the mailman had picked up the letter the next morning, I began looking for the coming of the camera. Each succeeding morning, around nine o'clock, I would clamber up the hemlock tree in front of the farmhouse and peer eastward down the road to catch the first glimpse of the little white, covered-in cart in which the rural-delivery mailman brought letters and parcels from Michigan City. Day after day I hastily slid down again, my hands and bare feet black with the pitch of the resinous trunk, and raced to the mailbox as the cart pulled up in front of Lone Oak. And each day, for more than a week, disappointment awaited me.

After the top of the white cart had disappeared over Gunder's Hill I used to wander about the farm and along the marsh-paths and through the north woods spotting birds' nests and rabbit forms and woodchuck holes. As I walked I made lists of the innumerable pictures I would take as soon as the box camera came. On the ninth day it arrived.

I opened the package in haste. Half a dozen times I read the instructions. I was appalled at the complexity of even this simple mechanism. In handling it I seemed, as Gramp would say, "as awkward as a cow on skates." Fully half an hour had passed before I felt sufficient confidence to load in the roll of film. When the back was snapped shut and the film wound to "Number 1," I set forth—a camera-hunter in reality.

Beside the ditch bordering the cherry orchard a young cottontail had made its form. I had been training it on previous days for just this moment. Time after time I had approached slowly and silently until I was no more than four or five feet away. Then I had lifted an imaginary camera and had clicked an imaginary shutter. The rabbit was used to my presence. It would sit motionless for minutes at a time, watching me with round, unblinking eyes, its veined ears lying flat along its back.

Camera in hand, I now moved cautiously toward the

cottontail. There was hardly a cloud in the sky. The sun was shining over my shoulder, just as the directions suggested. I squinted into the little rectangular window of the black box. The rabbit, sensing that something unusual was going on, lifted its ears. I pushed down the shutter-lever. At the metallic click, the cottontail was off, bolting away through the grass. But on my film, I felt sure, I had recorded a picture which would remain for years after the animal, itself, was no more.

Long before noon I had used my last film on a view of the house and the lone oak tree behind it. After dinner I picked strawberries with a fresh burst of enthusiasm. I realized that I would need many, many rolls of film to capture all the innumerable pictures I wanted to take.

I could hardly wait, that evening, for darkness to come. I read the instructions for developing the film over and over again. As soon as the supper dishes were washed, I laid my chemicals and trays out on the kitchen table and began hanging blankets over the windows. By half past eight it seemed dark enough to engage in the mysterious rite of photographic development.

First I mixed up my little packet of hypo and stirred into water the white powder from the tube of MQ developer. Then I lit a stub of a candle which fitted inside the red-cloth darkroom lantern. The dull reddish glow it emitted left me in almost complete darkness. I fumbled around for the roll of film, stripped off the paper, and began pumping the slippery strip up and down through the tray of developer. Eventually, against the dull glow of the red lantern, I was able to see thrilling evidences of pictures—lighter and darker patches on the film.

Although the strip, when finally dry, proved to be much over-developed and although black, light-struck patches marred the edges, the center section held pictures which we all could recognize. The rabbit, its ears erect and its round eyes alert, was the prize picture of the roll. It was the first of many thousand nature pictures which have provided interest and excitement during succeeding years.

My photographic fever continued all summer. I took under-exposed pictures in the depths of the north woods and over-exposed pictures in the glare of the sand-dunes. I snapped close-ups of moving animals and found only a blurred image on my film, and I photographed distant butterflies and saw them recorded no larger than pinheads on the resulting nega-tives. I learned by making mistakes.

There were so many pictures my box camera couldn't take, so many things too small to photograph or too fast to stop with a slow shutter speed, that disappointments mounted. However, even though only a small proportion of the hun-dreds of pictures I had seen vividly in my dreams ever materi-alized on film, the thrill of stalking wild creatures—camera in hand—and of seeing a long-desired picture take form before my eyes in the darkroom, left a lasting impression.

In later years other and better cameras followed this initial purchase. Each opened up new opportunities for close-ups or action shots. Each accompanied me on memorable trips afield, on expeditions that carried me tens of thousands of miles and resulted in a harvest of enjoyment as well as pic-tures. It was the black box of Lone Oak days—the camera that 20,000 strawberries purchased—that opened the door to all this later pleasure.

Born in Joliet, Illinois, **Edwin Way Teale** *spent many summers outside Valparaiso, Indiana. He grew up to be one of the country's most eminent nature writers and an accomplished photographer, pioneering new techniques for capturing close-up images of insects and other living things.*

Rain

ANTWONE QUENTON FISHER

*The summer of 1968 was a time of sadness and despair for Americans
following the assassinations of Martin Luther King Jr. and Robert F.
Kennedy, both peaceful crusaders for civil rights. Antwone Fisher, a foster
child living in an unloving household in Cleveland, felt all the weight of
the nation's struggles and his own that summer. But in this excerpt from
his memoir,* Finding Fish, *he recounts a turning point in the season of
grief.*

Same summer, not much time later, close to my ninth birth-
day, it's a muggy, overcast Saturday after cartoons, after house-
work. The smell in the air promises rain, but judging from the
medium gray of the sky, I think I can make it to Mr. Murphy's
and back before it starts to fall. No one around upstairs, I steal
another nickel from myself out of my Clabber Girl baking
powder can bank in Mizz Pickett's room and slip out of the
house unnoticed. Barefoot, dressed in a crewneck shirt and
cargo shorts with zippers on the pockets, I run up our block
and over to 105. The thunder rumblings begin. Just God moving around his furniture, that's what Flo likes to say, even
though the big booming sound scares me a little.

At Mr. Murphy's I buy five Smarties rolls, little sweet tarts
wrapped in cellophane, and unroll them into my pockets,

leaving one pocket unzipped enough to stick two fingers in so I can eat the candy piece by piece on the return trip.

Halfway home, the sky goes from dark gray to almost black and a loud thunder snap accompanies the first few raindrops that fall. Heavy, warm, big drops, they drench me in seconds, like an overturned bucket from the sky dumping just on my head. I reach my hands up and out, as if that can stop my getting wetter, and open my mouth, trying to swallow the downpour, till it finally hits me how funny it is, my trying to stop the rain.

This is so funny to me, I laugh and laugh, as loud and free as I want. Instead of hurrying to higher ground, I jump lower, down off the curb, splashing through the puddles, playing and laughing all the way home. In all my life till now, rain has meant staying inside and not being able to go out to play. But now for the first time I realize that rain doesn't have to be bad. And what's more, I understand, sadness doesn't have to be bad, either. Come to think of it, I figure you need sadness, just as you need the rain.

Thoughts and ideas pour through my awareness. It feels to me that happiness is almost scary, like how I imagine being drunk might feel—real silly and not caring what anybody else says. Plus, that happy feeling always leaves so fast, and you know it's going to go before it even does. Sadness lasts longer, making it more familiar, and more comfortable. But maybe, I wonder, there's a way to find some happiness in the sadness. After all, it's like the rain, something you can't avoid. And so, it seems to me, if you're caught in it, you might as well try to make the best of it.

Getting caught in the warm, wet deluge that particular day in that terrible summer full of wars and fires that made no sense was a wonderful thing to have happen. It taught me to understand rain, not to dread it. There were going to be days, I knew, when it would pour without warning, days when I'd find myself without an umbrella. But my understanding would act as my all-purpose slicker and rubber boots. It was preparing me for stormy weather, arming me with the knowledge that no matter how hard it seemed, it couldn't rain forever. At some point, I knew, it would come to an end.

Antwone Quenton Fisher currently lives and writes in California. In addition to writing Finding Fish, *he wrote the screenplay for* Antwone Fisher, *a movie based on the memoir. The film was produced by Denzel Washington and released in theaters in 2002.*

Great Northern Pike

KATHARINE CRAWFORD ROBEY

Northern pike are distributed widely across the Great Lakes region. Voracious predators, they eat everything from other fish to leeches to muskrats, and put on weight more quickly than most other fish. Their large size is one reason they're a popular target for lake fishermen throughout the region.

All that July, John awoke at dawn to the low sounds of his father preparing to fish. There was the clatter of rods, the thud of the screen door, the creaking of the wheel that lowered the boat into Platte Lake. From his bed on the screened porch he'd listen until the whine of the motor faded away. He longed to go with him. Through the binoculars he could sometimes make him out, hunched over in the pale gray light, a solitary figure in the middle of the lake.

At night while the fire threw tall shadows over the mellow log walls of the cabin, John watched his dad change lures and sinkers, talking of the old days and huge muskies. He talked of stringers so full of fish that two grown men had to hold them up. "Nothing but three-pound bass out there now," his dad would say to his mother, shaking his head. "The lake's all fished out." But each time his dad said it, John wanted even more to go with him. He knew he'd bring him luck.

How do you say you're ready to fish with the experts at dawn? How do you put it when yours is a serious fishing family, your dad known as the best fisherman on the lake since his father before him? John's dad hadn't been allowed in a fishing boat until he'd turned sixteen. John was only ten.

Then one morning toward the beginning of August when John heard his father's footsteps crossing the porch near his bed, he sat up. "Take me with you," he blurted out. "I've been casting off the dock. I caught a bass."

His father looked at him in surprise. He was a quiet man and in the summertime John figured his mind was so filled with fishing that he didn't much notice him. His dad hesitated. "You'd have to wear a life jacket." He glanced outside. "Looks like rain. We won't stay long."

The boat glided to a stop in the middle of the lake. John peered through the mist. There, etched in gray, were the three pine trees that towered above the bluffs of the north shore, marking the bass hole. They were in his father's favorite fishing spot. In summers past his dad had brought back stringers of five-pound bass from here and pike, too—northern pike so enormous that his father said they'd dragged his bobber underwater a foot. Then even he'd jumped to his feet, shouting with excitement. Shivers ran through John.

"Bait your line," his dad said in a serious voice.

Some of the thrill faded from John. He carefully lifted up the bait bucket, trying not to bang it against the side of the boat. He grabbed a slippery minnow, slipped the hook through, then plopped his line into the still, gray-green water.

He heard the swish of a fly line and glanced back. His father had already set out a heavy pole for pike. It was propped against the stern. He was standing up, casting for bass with dry flies. John watched the line move in perfect rhythm across the water. His dad made it look so easy. Teach me that, John wanted to say. But the man seemed so imposing, so much as if he didn't want to be disturbed, that John sat back, silent. Contenting himself with the play of his line, he waited.

A loon cried near the west end. The mist closed in on them and small drops of water splashed into the lake and on the rim of John's hat. He worried that his father would take him in without giving the fishing a chance. But there was no thunder and lightning, just a quiet morning rain. His dad kept casting.

After a while the rain passed and the fog began to lift, leaving the water a dull, flat gray. John glanced at his dad's bobber. It was barely moving, the water was so still. He wished his dad would catch a pike. He'd heard him talk of the thrill before. He longed to ask what it was like. But he didn't know whether expert fishermen spoke much in the boat. He shifted in his seat.

Quick, light nibbles focused his attention on his line. He reeled in a small perch, not large enough to keep. He threw it back in, baited his hook with a worm, and cast his line far out over the drop off. It was a good cast. His practicing had paid off. But if his dad saw it, he said nothing. The only attention John attracted was that of a seagull. It wheeled out of the mist and landed near the boat, waiting for handouts.

The sun came out and the mist disappeared. The water turned sparkling blue. "It's been an hour," his dad said. "I haven't had a bite. You've only caught a perch. Want to go in?"

"Not yet," John said.

His father nodded and rowed them farther out. "Here," he said, dipping his hand into the bait bucket. "Try this sucker instead of your worm."

"But that's too big," said John. "Only a pike would hit that."

His father shrugged and smiled slightly. "Who knows. Might as well use up the bait. You never know."

John turned from him and let the sucker down into the water with hard jerks. He didn't know how to catch a pike. You could only catch perch and small bass off the dock. His father knew that. Maybe all he really cared about was using up the bait! John propped his rod across the sides of the boat and pulled his fishing hat down to hide his eyes.

Suddenly his line shot out with a zing. Startled, he lunged for the rod just as it was being pulled overboard. He leaped to his feet.

"Dad!" he shouted.

"Wait!" his father cried, jumping up, too, and rocking the boat. "Wait until the fish stops running! Then set the hook!"

John had never seen his dad excited like this. Breathless, John waited, watching the line spin out. Finally the whining reel stopped and he yanked up on the pole. "It feels like there's only a dead weight on my line," he said.

"Maybe the sucker's just stuck in some weeds," his dad said, still standing. "Then again, maybe not."

The reel gave out a shrill whine. John felt a heavy pull on his line. The tip of his rod began to dip and arch in and out of the water as if the pole itself were alive.

"Keep the tip of your rod out of the water," his dad said.

John tried to lift up the pole, but it was bent almost double and the tip was two feet underwater. His hands were shaking, but he managed to loosen the tension on the line by turning a screw on the reel. The whining became less shrill. The tip of the rod came up. Suddenly John's line relaxed and the tension disappeared altogether. His heart sank to his knees. "I've lost him!" he cried, sitting down.

Off the bow of the boat a fish broke water and jumped. It was a great northern pike and it stood on its tail, shining in the sunlight like a green sea god.

"Did you see that fish jump!" John cried.

"Yes!" his father cried back. "That's *your* fish!"

John started and jumped to his feet. The pike dove underwater. He felt a heavy pull on his rod and his stomach lurched within him. It was the pike.

"Look!" his dad shouted, pointing at the water.

Under the surface John saw a flash of white—ghostlike against the green. Then the fish disappeared.

"He's driving for the bottom," his father said. "That's what the big ones do. Don't try to wind him in too fast. Play the fish."

John's line spun out. He had to loosen the tension again or risk that the rod would snap. Slowly, he began to reel in the pike. After what seemed like a long time he saw again the flash of white. Long minutes passed. Beads of perspiration stung his eyes. The taste of salt reached his lips.

His dad peered into the water. "Fish has got to be getting tired by now."

"I'm tired," John cried. His arms were trembling from exertion. "I can't do it, Dad. You bring him in."

"It's your fish, John. You catch him." His father's voice was hoarse.

At last John began to see the pike more clearly. Dark green mixed with flashing white, twisting, bending, magnified to huge proportions by the water. "He's coming up!" John shouted. His legs were shaking. The pike looked like it was about three feet long, mottled green on darker green. The fish began to coast smoothly upward, almost as if it were assisting John.

"You've exhausted him," his dad said. "Bring him alongside the boat. Slowly now. Don't let him bang the hook out against the side."

John extended his pole as far out over the water as he could without falling overboard himself. He brought the pike closer. It did indeed seem tired. The fish came into full view. Its snout was long and its body lean. Its tail was spotted brown. It was the most magnificent pike John had ever seen. He felt triumphant. But he'd heard how a fish could rest like his was now, then bolt again for the bottom. John didn't have the strength to bring the pike back up again.

"Get the net, get the net, Dad."

Out of the corner of his eye he saw his dad bend down and look under the seats. He glanced at John strangely, hesitating. "Where is it?" he asked.

John's heart stopped. In his mind he saw the net clearly, lying on the pine table in the living room where his dad had been mending it. His dad had asked him to take the net down to the boat that morning.

"I left it on the table," he heard himself say. For a second everything around him stood perfectly still, his dad, the clouds, the seagull nearby. He stared at the pike lying calmly in the water next to the boat—regaining its strength. John felt desperate. He must have that fish, the first big fish he'd ever caught.

Maybe he could simply haul it in over the edge. But he knew the line would break. Maybe he could grab it with his bare hands. But he knew the slippery fish would dart away. Maybe his dad could start the motor and drag it to shore. But he knew his father would never do that. It was not sportsman-like to drown a fish.

He glanced at his father. How stupid he must think I am. How unlike a real fisherman. How unlike him. Tears were hot in his eyes. He tried to brush them away.

Then came his father's steady voice, "I've forgotten the net more than once myself. Even grown men cry when they lose a fish like that." For some reason he began to unbutton his shirt. "But you haven't lost him yet."

For a dizzying moment, John thought that his dad didn't care at all about his ruined victory, that he was simply taking off his shirt to get a suntan. But then his dad dipped the shirt into the water on the opposite side of the boat from the pike and twisted it into a sort of cradle. Immediately John saw what his father had in mind, saw that his father knew how much he wanted the pike.

"Take the long end of the shirt," his dad said. "I can't pull in a fish like that alone."

With shaking hands John clicked his reel to locked position and propped the rod under the seat. He took one end of the wet shirt. His dad held the other. At a nod from his father, they slid it quietly, smoothly, deeply below the resting pike.

John's heart began to leap wildly as if it would jump out of his chest and be the thing to scare the fish away forever. But he must be calm.

His dad glanced at him. "Now!" he cried.

Almost as if they were one, they hoisted up the shirt and flipped the pike over the side of the boat. Immediately it came to life, thrashing its tail and jumping about near their feet.

John sat down, panting, and stared at the beautiful fish. His father took a stringer, ran it through the pike's gills and tied it securely to an oar lock. In the water again, the pike loomed as large as ever, but now it swam calmly beside the boat almost as if it were tame.

His dad broke the silence. "You're quite a fisherman," he said.

John glanced away from the pike and looked at his father. The wind had risen and he thought his father must be cold without a shirt on. But his dad didn't seem to mind the breeze. He was smiling. "We'll have to remember the net tomorrow," he was saying. "You're coming in the morning, aren't you? Looks like there's room in the boat for two."

As a child, **Katharine Crawford Robey** *spent her winters on a farm in Wisconsin and her summers in a log cabin on Platte Lake. There she fished for bass and pike with her father. The ending of "Great Northern Pike," Robey says, is true. Though she now lives in Atlanta, Georgia, she still visits Platte Lake every summer.*

Wild Lives

The Raccoon Brigade

PAT KERTZMAN

Raccoons are among the most adaptable of mammals. Though their original habitat consisted primarily of undisturbed woodlands, they have learned to thrive in urban and suburban areas, leading what is usually a peaceful coexistence with the local human population.

For a long time we lived in peace with the raccoons. Their home was a clump of hollow trees across the street. They were like intriguing cousins from another country, our non-English-speaking relatives.

Sometimes Mom let me leave a bowl of leftovers behind the garage for them. They gobbled up vegetables, casseroles, fish, cereal, nuts, fruit, sweets—just about anything. I made sure we supplied all the major food groups. The neighbors complained of raccoons raiding their garbage cans in the middle of the night, but they never touched ours. We had an understanding.

My sister Carla took a picture of the giant raccoon we called Hugo shucking an ear of corn. He clamped the ear between his hind feet and removed every leaf and strand with his nimble little hands. Hugo was concentrating so hard that he hardly blinked when the camera flashed. Carla captioned the snapshot "Butter would be perfect."

Carla and I named each new kit and kept a record of births and deaths. We got their personalities down on paper, too. You might think raccoons are all pretty much the same. It isn't true. Adrienne had a large, pointy mask and a scraggly tail. Maxwell limped and had a bald gouge in his side. Hugo was gigantic and fearless—always first at the dinner bowl and last to leave. He'd growl and skirmish over a piece of scrambled egg. Molly was happy and flirtatious. She chirped and trilled and purred whenever we looked at her. Her mother sometimes dragged her away by the scruff, scolding all the way.

In the Year of the Raccoons, Carla was thirteen, I was eleven, and our brother Samuel was two. Our dogs, Garrison the boxer and Murphy the dalmatian, were young and spunky. The raccoons' midnight escapades sent Murphy into furious growling and howling. "Don't you care what's happening here?" she'd bark accusingly. "We're losing control!"

On summer nights when it was too hot to sleep, the whole family would go out with a lantern to look at the raccoons.

Samuel would quietly ponder the moon, the trees full of eyes, and the lantern-cast shadows. Then two things happened that changed everything.

Samuel was growing and needed a room of his own, so Dad helped another man turn our attic into a living area. All that was left above it was a crawl space. Around the same time, the village council decided that Grange Avenue was too busy and congested and should be expanded. The old trees were chopped down before we could protest. Forever there, gone in a day. Where would the raccoon families go? Not too far, we hoped.

Carla started hearing noises at night above her room. She had an active imagination, so my parents assured her, "Go to sleep; it's nothing." Eventually everyone heard something, but we were too busy to investigate the noise.

One wet Saturday in April, Mom and Dad noticed a hole in the back of the house leading to the crawl space. They raced into the house and headed straight for the stairway. They crawled through the grungy space like crocodiles on a mission and found a litter of four kits bawling for supper. Mother Raccoon was nowhere to be seen.

My parents emerged from the crawl space dirty and damp and wondering what to do. "Let's call the DNR," Mom suggested. The man at the Department of Natural Resources said that this sort of thing happened often in Wisconsin. Apparently raccoons got tired of waiting for warm, dry weather too. He suggested removing the kits and placing them in a shallow container in the yard. Adult raccoons would most likely retrieve them. Then we should board up the hole. The raccoons would get the message and stay away. I was proud that the raccoons had used our house for a nursery and sorry that they couldn't stay.

"They're wild and they always will be," Dad said when I argued.

"Neighbors are one thing, live-ins are another," Mom added.

Mom and Dad boarded up the hole tightly with lumber and metal fencing. We cleaned a shallow tub from the garage and lined it with an old yellow blanket. We placed the kits inside and left them oatmeal with milk and cooked apples. We covered them up and hoped for the best. Nobody said anything, but I'm sure we all feared that a hawk, fox, or neighborhood hound would find them first.

I kept Murphy and Garrison away from the babies. I could tell Murphy thought we were cracked for keeping baby raccoons in a tub in the backyard. "Your opinion doesn't count," I informed her. She cocked her head in complete disagreement.

"We're doing the right thing," Mom told the wall as we picked at our supper in silence. Even Samuel was quiet.

The next day the kits were gone. The yellow blanket looked lonely in the tub, speckled by the morning sun. Raccoon prints were everywhere.

Late that night an incredible racket woke me up. I flew out of bed, grabbed my robe, and met Carla in the hall. Mom and Dad were already up. Dad turned the floodlights on, and we all ran to the backyard. Neighbors were gathering. Mouths moved and brows wrinkled in alarm, but we couldn't hear a word. The screeches were deafening.

One by one, eleven adult raccoons scaled the back of our house. The journey was treacherous, but they were expert climbers. They marched with purpose and spoke in raging tongues. The raccoons took turns working at the patched hole for over an hour—clawing, scratching, biting, instructing, and criticizing each other. Their efforts were impressive, but they only managed to ruin some of our siding. Finally they climbed down in orderly single file, as if they'd rehearsed, and walked away. They kept their backs to us. We were newly despicable, undeserving of a glance. Only one turned around for a final hiss. Then they were gone.

The neighbors stood around wondering at the spectacle. Why so many raccoons? Carla and I agreed that most of them were new to us. We had recognized only two. The raccoons must have recruited friends and cousins, aunts and uncles, even grandraccoons. It was a complete raccoon brigade. But why the loud protest?

We thought we might know.

The next morning Dad and I crept into the crawl space and listened. Sure enough, a kit was huddled in a corner, mewing pitifully. We'd overlooked it, but the raccoons hadn't.

"You are one missed little kit," Dad told it.

It was damp and frosty that night. We covered the kit with blankets, and I worried like a new mother. Would it suffocate or freeze? Would that mongrel down the street who roamed at night find it first? How persistent are raccoons? I wondered. Would the search party return, or would they consider their duty done and hope gone?

Sometime that night, the woebegone kit was claimed from the tub. They were quiet this time, but footprints showed the raccoon brigade had returned.

We never saw our raccoon friends again, but I think of them often. I'm writing this so Samuel can remember, too. I wonder if new kids are keeping track of births and deaths and food groups. Even if no one is, it's all right. The raccoons will go on. They have each other.

Ever since **Pat Kertzman** *was a child, writing has been one of her greatest joys. Most of her stories are realistic and involve animals. She's been published in magazines, textbooks, and on a website.*

An Evening on Isle Royale

MARY BARTLETT CASKEY

At dusk we watched
a moose forage
for a cache of salad
in a swampy bog
close to Hidden Lake
where old-timers insist
you go if you haven't
yet happened on the goal
of every Isle visitor: moose.

Her brown hulk
trapped the last rays
of sunlight against a crowd
of balsam deadheads,
her forelegs were splayed
like a giraffe, and the dangling
bell of her throat just
skimmed the water.
When she lifted her long face,

green lilies dripped from her chin.
The distance between us
was so short

we could see the majesty
of her brown mass,
the veil of her shyness,
a carnival of an appetite,
and enormous joy in the long full snort
that dismissed our presence.

A retired educator, **Mary Bartlett Caskey** *lives near Rockford, Illinois, in woods she shares with wild turkeys, downy woodpeckers, raccoons, and her husband, David. She is a graduate of Swarthmore College and has published her poetry in many magazines. She spends part of each summer in a cabin on Isle Royale.*

Four Skinny Trees

SANDRA CISNEROS

In her novel The House on Mango Street, *Sandra Cisneros portrays the world of a young girl named Esperanza Cordero and her family. The Corderos have just bought their first home, a ramshackle house in an impoverished Chicago neighborhood. In this excerpt, Esperanza shares her thoughts about the four trees that grow outside her new home.*

They are the only ones who understand me. I am the only one who understands them. Four skinny trees with skinny necks and pointy elbows like mine. Four who do not belong here but are here. Four raggedy excuses planted by the city. From our room we can hear them, but Nenny just sleeps and doesn't appreciate these things.

Their strength is secret. They send ferocious roots beneath the ground. They grow up and they grow down and grab the earth between their hairy toes and bite the sky with violent teeth and never quit their anger. This is how they keep.

Let one forget his reason for being, they'd all droop like tulips in a glass, each with their arms around the other. Keep, keep, keep, trees say when I sleep. They teach.

When I am too sad and too skinny to keep keeping, when I am a tiny thing against so many bricks, then it is I look at trees. When there is nothing left to look at on this street. Four who grew despite concrete. Four who reach and do not forget to reach. Four whose only reason is to be and be.

Sandra Cisneros *grew up in Chicago and Mexico, and attended Loyola University and the University of Iowa's Writers' Workshop. She is the author of numerous works of fiction and poetry, including* The House on Mango Street *and* Woman Hollering Creek and Other Stories.

A Bear in the Backyard

JACK BECKLUND

When Jack Becklund and his wife, Patti, moved to a home in rural Grand Marais, Minnesota, they didn't know anything about bears. But one day a young yearling bear ambled up onto their back porch and started eating the sunflower seeds they had put out for the birds. In time, the Becklunds formed an extraordinary relationship with this bear, whom they called Little Bit, and with other bears in the region. Although they gained fascinating insights into the lives of black bears, their actions are not meant to be a model for others. Readers are reminded to treat bears and all wild animals with respect and caution.

The next morning Patti washed several loads of clothes and hung them outside. It promised to be another glorious and sunny day. A while later, she noticed that two of the cats, Caesar and Einstein, were sitting on the dining room table, looking out the window in the direction of the clothesline.

At first she paid no attention. Then, seeing that the cats continued to sit there watching, she glanced out. "I don't see anything," she said to them. "What are you guys watching so intently?"

At noon, she went out to check the clothes and bring in those that were dry. As she started to work, she noticed a gap on the line where something was obviously missing. She thought about it briefly, then it hit her. The pink bathrobe was gone. It was thick and comfy. Her favorite.

The clothesline was near the woods, so she walked over and looked around. Then she came inside and called for me to come out. "Someone has taken my pink bathrobe, and I intend to find it. You go that way, and I'll try over here."

We split up and I went into the woods, where I looked for several minutes before giving up and returning to the lawn. Moments later, Patti emerged on the other side of the yard, carrying her bathrobe. "I'm gonna spank that bear," she said, explaining that someone had pulled the bathrobe down, carried it into the woods, then used it to soften a daybed in the tall grass. Whoever had used it had left a small whorl of black fur as evidence.

"Any other damage to it?" I asked.

"No, I guess I'm lucky it's still in one piece."

She took the bathrobe inside and rewashed it. When she hung it up, she anchored it to the line with four clothespins. Twice in the next hour she checked it. Twice it was still there. The third time it was still there, and the fourth. Maybe, she thought, the idea of using her bathrobe as a bed liner had been forgotten.

A while later, she went out to bring in the last of the wash, which should by now be dry. The bathrobe was gone. "Oh no, not again," she wailed.

With several of the windows open, I heard her clearly and hustled outside in time to see her striding straight for the spot where the daybeds were located. This time, she caught the culprit red-handed.

"Shame on you, Little Bit. That's my bathrobe, not yours," she said. By now Little Bit was up and retreating from her pink-lined bed.

I met Patti emerging with the bathrobe again in hand. "Little Bit?" I asked.

She nodded. "Who else? At least she didn't seem to harm it any." After being washed for the third time that day, the furry robe—found to be still in good condition—was tumbled dry in the basement dryer.

That same evening, we were outside on the deck feeding chipmunks. Our friend Chester was there, squabbling with his cousins while filling his cheeks with nuts. Little Bit arrived and climbed ponderously up the stairs to the deck. She strode straight through the swirl of chipmunks, paying no attention, and went right over to Patti, who gathered a small pile of almonds for her on the bench.

Little Bit ignored the nuts and nuzzled Patti's hand, as she often did when she wanted to be hand-fed. Sometimes she absolutely would not eat them in any other way. This was one of those days.

Patti picked up the nuts she had placed on the bench. Because of very low blood pressure, she'd become dizzy and her hand was shaking. Little Bit saw her hand trembling and did something totally unexpected. She lifted her large paw, cupped it beneath Patti's hand, and actually held her hand steady while gently picking the nuts up with her mouth.

Patti said nothing, but she understood, and her eyes filled with tears. She stroked the big bear's neck and turned away. It was a special moment, one that we could never have predicted and that we would never forget.

Jack Becklund has worked in advertising and the newspaper business. He currently lives with his wife, Patti, in New Smyrna Beach, Florida.

Hummingbird

PAMELA USCHUK

Slashed into the rufous chest,
a throat like a chunk of neon ruby
gives him away as he whirs
to his mate perched in blackberry brambles
spread beneath our windows.
Thief of sunlight,
spangled,
pure infrared,
hummingbird shakes kinetic wings
and he is off.
No sloth, he revs to fifth gear.
Torqued so high, he
does not fly so much
as bee buzz
straight lines stunning air
or diving to stab at us
who wander close
to his intended nest.
We whose imaginations only reach
such velocity confronting
possibilities
like fame or anger or love,
must watch, amazed,

at lightning's bloody jewel.
Hummingbird, tongue-sized,
bright articulator of spirits,
you attack all intruders,
hawks and wrens alike.
Even from shadows, you
manufacture light.
Teach us your courage these days
when mist takes the world,
your tenderness as you take rare rest,
yawn, then shiver
in your perfect wings
daring such gravity as finally grounds us.

Pamela Uschuk *is the author of two books,* Finding Peaches in the Desert *and* One-Legged Dancer, *and the director of the Center for Women Writers at Salem College in Winston-Salem, North Carolina. This poem was written about a hummingbird she encountered in Traverse City, Michigan, where she lived for nine years.*

The Turtle

GEORGE VUKELICH

Snapping turtles inhabit freshwater lakes and streams throughout Wisconsin and other states in the Great Lakes region. Although they are vulnerable as hatchlings, those that survive to adulthood have very few predators except humans. They are estimated to live an average of thirty to forty years in the wild, and often grow to be as much as forty to sixty pounds.

They were driving up to fish the White Creek for German Browns and the false dawn was purpling the Wisconsin countryside when they spotted the huge humpbacked object in the middle of the sand road, and Jimmy coasted the station wagon to a stop.

"Pa," he said. "Turtle. Lousy snapper."

Old Tony sat up. "Is he dead?"

"Not yet," Jimmy said. "Not yet he isn't." He shifted into neutral and pulled the hand brake. The snapper lay large and dark green in the headlight beams, and they got out and went around to look at it closely. The turtle moved a little and left razorlike claw marks in the wet sand, and it waited.

"Probably heading for the creek," Jimmy said. "They kill trout like crazy."

They stood staring down.

"I'd run the wagon over him," Jimmy said. "Only he's too big."

He looked around and walked to the ditchway and came back with a long, finger-thick pine branch. He jabbed it into the turtle's face, and the snake head lashed out and struck like spring steel, and the branch snapped like a stick of macaroni, and it all happened fast as a match flare.

"Look-a that!" Tony whistled.

"You bet, Pa. I bet he goes sixty pounds. Seventy maybe."

The turtle was darting its head around now in long stretching movements.

"I think he got some branch stuck in his craw," Jimmy said. He got out a cigarette and lit it and flipped the match at the rock-green shell.

"I wish now I'd brought the twenty-two," he said. "The pistol."

"You going to kill him?"

"Why not?" Jimmy asked. "They kill trout, don't they?"

They stood there smoking and not talking and looking down at the unmoving shell.

"I could use the lug wrench on him," Jimmy said. "Only I don't think it's long enough. I don't want my hands near him."

Tony didn't say anything.

"You watch him," Jimmy said. "I'll go find something in the wagon."

Slowly Tony squatted down onto his haunches and smoked and stared at the turtle. Poor Old One, he thought. You had the misfortune to be caught in the middle of a sand road, and you are very vulnerable on the sand roads, and now you are going to get the holy life beaten out of you.

The turtle stopped its stretching movements and was still. Tony looked at the full webbed feet and the nail claws, and he knew the truth.

"It would be different in the water, turtle," he said. "In the water you could cut down anybody."

He thought about this snapper in the water and how it would move like a torpedo and bring down trout, and nobody would monkey with it in the water—and here it was in the middle of a sand road, vulnerable as a baby and waiting to get its brains beaten out.

He finished his cigarette and field-stripped it and got to his feet and walked to the wagon and reached into the glove compartment for the thermos of coffee. What was he getting all worked up about a turtle for? He was an old man and he was acting like a kid, and they were going up to the White for German Browns, and he was getting worked up about a godforsaken turtle in the middle of a godforsaken sand road. *Godforsaken.* He walked back to the turtle and hunched down and sipped at the strong black coffee and watched the old snapper watching him.

Jimmy came up to him, holding the bumper jack.

"I want to play it safe," he said. "I don't think the lug wrench is long enough." He squatted beside Tony. "What do you think?"

"He waits," Tony said. "What difference what I think?"

Jimmy squinted at him.

"I can tell something's eating you. What are you thinking, Pa?"

"I am thinking this is not a brave thing."

"What?"

"This turtle—he does not have a chance."

Jimmy lit a cigarette and hefted the bumper jack. The turtle moved ever so slightly.

"You talk like an old woman. An old tired woman."

"I can understand this turtle's position."

"He doesn't have a chance?"

"That's right."

"And that bothers you?"

Tony looked into Jimmy's face.

"That is right," he said. "That bothers me."

"Well of all the dumb stupid things," Jimmy said. "What do you want me to do? Get down on all fours and fight with him?"

"No," Tony said. "Not on all fours. Not on all fours." He looked at Jimmy. "In the water. Fight this turtle in the water. That would be a brave thing, my son."

Jimmy put down the bumper jack and reached for the thermos jug and didn't say anything. He drank his coffee and smoked his cigarette and he stared at the turtle and didn't say anything.

"You're crazy," he said finally.

"It is a thought, my son. A thought. This helpless plodding old one like a little baby in this sand road, eh? But in the water, his home . . ." Tony snapped his fingers with the suddenness of a switchblade. "In the water he could cut down anyone, anything . . . any man. Fight him in the water, Jimmy. Use your bumper jack in the water . . ."

"I think you're nuts," Jimmy said. "I think you're honest-to-goodness nuts."

Tony shrugged. "This does not seem fair to you, eh? To be in the water with this one." He motioned at the turtle. "This seems nuts to you. Crazy to you. Because in the water, you are not a match."

"What are you trying to prove, Pa?"

"Jimmy. This turtle is putting up his life. In the road here, you are putting up nothing. You have nothing to lose at all. Not a finger or a hand or your life. Nothing. You smash him with a long steel bumper jack, and he cannot get to you. He has as much chance as a ripe watermelon."

"So?"

"So I want you to put up something, also. You should have something to lose, or it is no match."

Jimmy looked at the old man and then at the turtle.

"Any fool can smash a watermelon," Tony said. "It does not take a brave man."

"Pa. It's only a turtle. You're making a federal case."

Old Tony looked at his son. "All right," he said. "Finish your coffee now and do what you are going to do. I say nothing more. Only for the next five minutes, put yourself into this turtle's place. Put yourself into his shell and watch through his eyes. And try to think what he is thinking when he sees a coward coming to kill him with a long steel bumper jack."

Jimmy got to his feet and ground out his cigarette.

"All right, Pa," he said. "All right. You win."

Tony rose slowly from his crouch.

"No," he said. "Not me. You. You win."

"But, Pa, they do kill trout."

"So," Tony said. "They kill trout. Nature put them here,

and they kill trout. To survive. The trout are not extinct, eh? We kill trout, also, we men. To survive? No, for sport. This Old One, he takes what he needs. I do not kill him for being in nature's plan. I do not play God."

Jimmy walked to the rear of the wagon then and flung down the bumper jack and closed up the door and came back.

"Pa," he said. "Honest-to-goodness, you got the nuttiest ideas I ever heard."

Old Tony walked around behind the snapper and gently prodded it with his boot toe, and the turtle went waddling forward across the road and toppled over the sand shoulder and disappeared in the brushy growth of the creek bank. Tony and his son climbed into the wagon and sat looking at each other. The sun was coming up strong now, and the sky was cracking open like a shell and spilling reds and golds and blues, and Jimmy started the engine.

George Vukelich *was a well-known Wisconsin writer and the author of such books as* Song of the Ouisconsing *and* North Country Notebook.

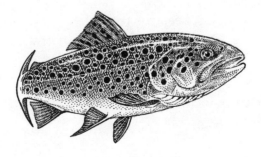

Crows

JILL BARRIE

When the leaves fall,
you see limbs of trees

and dead twiggy nests
resting in them.

The wind blows incessantly,
branches bow,

and enormous crows
fold their broad wings

and perch within
the thin skeletons.

They are the beating
black hearts

that keep the trees alive
through the empty plain of winter.

Jill Barrie *has published poems in a variety of magazines. She lives in Naperville, Illinois.*

Shorthand on the Snow

January 1 to February 15

LOUIS W. CAMPBELL
WITH CLAIRE GAVIN

During the cold winter months, many animals retreat into dens and burrows. But as naturalist Louis Campbell explains in this essay, winter is an especially good time to follow the tracks of those animals that stay active above ground, and a time when he has often been rewarded by extremely strange wildlife sightings!

In winter, the marsh itself is barren and desolate. Cattails, reeds, and long grasses are a brown, whispering sea tossed by an icy wind. In open places, drifting snow piles up in ridges against the cattails. There are few signs of life, since food is extremely scarce. Only an occasional mound of vegetation, like a miniature igloo, indicates that muskrats are still here. Sometimes a set of tracks can be seen in the snow, where a hungry muskrat left its shelter in search of food. The staggered prints are distinctive: wide-spread toes border the reversed curved line left by a dragging tail. The only other indications that last summer's cattail village was a thriving community are the oval, bulky nests of marsh wrens and the neater structures of red-winged blackbirds, now capped with snow.

But the brushy borders of the marsh, the

weed-grown dikes, and the occasional patches of neighboring swamp forest provide living quarters for many kinds of wildlife. Sandwiched between the frozen marsh and the bare, open fields of the farms crowding the wetlands, they form a sanctuary for hard-pressed birds and mammals. Here food is plentiful: seeds, nuts, acorns, and wild fruits such as grape and sumac. Numerous shrubs, together with the arched tangles of last summer's tall weeds, provide birds and mammals with shelter from the cold and protection from their enemies.

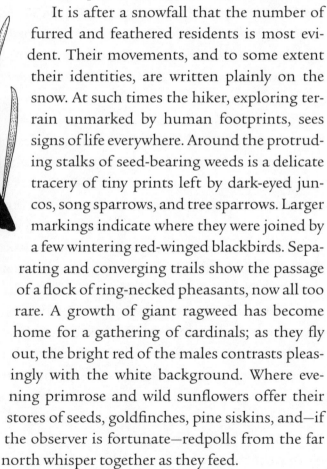

It is after a snowfall that the number of furred and feathered residents is most evident. Their movements, and to some extent their identities, are written plainly on the snow. At such times the hiker, exploring terrain unmarked by human footprints, sees signs of life everywhere. Around the protruding stalks of seed-bearing weeds is a delicate tracery of tiny prints left by dark-eyed juncos, song sparrows, and tree sparrows. Larger markings indicate where they were joined by a few wintering red-winged blackbirds. Separating and converging trails show the passage of a flock of ring-necked pheasants, now all too rare. A growth of giant ragweed has become home for a gathering of cardinals; as they fly out, the bright red of the males contrasts pleasingly with the white background. Where evening primrose and wild sunflowers offer their stores of seeds, goldfinches, pine siskins, and—if the observer is fortunate—redpolls from the far north whisper together as they feed.

The most common mammal tracks are the two-dot, two-dash of the cottontail rabbit, progressing through the courses of its dinner: first, seeds from locust pods; next, kernels of spiny cockleburs; finally, to top off the meal, bark gnawed from willow saplings. Where the underlying grass is thick, the snow is covered with tiny tracks of voles, or short-tailed meadow mice, sometimes ending in a tunnel.

I once came upon a vole that had evidently been feeding on fermented hawthorn berries. It was trudging round and round, marking out a three-foot circle in the snow, so intent that it didn't look up as I approached. When I picked it up, it squirmed and squeaked but, contrary to a vole's normally feisty nature, made no move to bite my fingers. Back on the ground, it was quiet for a moment, then found its former track and resumed the same slow, dogged circling. I was familiar with the behavior of cedar waxwings after eating fermented mountain ash berries, but this was my first encounter with a drunken mammal.

In wooded areas the vole's place is taken by the gentle white-footed mouse, sometimes confused with the deer mouse. It is a good climber, often making its winter home in a well-preserved bird's nest, which it covers over with grasses. If a watcher is cautious and moves slowly, he can disturb this velvet-eyed, long-tailed mouse just enough to coax it from its warm lair. Sometimes it will move only a few inches before clinging to a nearby twig, and will allow its tail to be touched. For some reason difficult to explain, a man feels very close to nature when a small wild creature curls its tail around his finger.

The path of a night-prowling raccoon is easily tracked by the marks of its distinctive hind paws, which have been compared to the feet of a human baby. But the opossum's trail is more difficult to decipher, its footprints irregular and haphazard as if it were returning from an all-night party. In contrast, skunk trails appear to be made soberly, carefully and deliberately, showing every claw, as one would expect from an animal with all the assurance in the world. Squirrel tracks are common in the woodlots, showing plainly where a fox squirrel has left its den in a hollow tree, crossed the snow, and dug out a nut or acorn buried weeks before. And weaving everywhere, in and out of the thickets, through the woods and over paths on top of the dikes, are the evenly spaced, precision-made tracks of the red fox, one foot set methodically ahead of the other.

A special discovery is a series of opposite markings imprinted at comparatively wide-spaced intervals. These could have been made only by a mink. One can almost picture it leaping sinuously over the snow as it leaves its home under a stump on the canal bank, looking for a mouse, a wandering muskrat, or an unwary short-tailed shrew.

Although the mink is pictured as a most efficient predator, ounce for ounce and inch for inch the short-tailed shrew and its smaller relative, the old field shrew, make the mink seem as harmless as a rabbit. The larger shrew *(Blarina b. brevicauda)* weighs an ounce and measures six inches plus a one-inch tail. The smaller shrew *(Cryptotis parva)* is three and a half inches and half an ounce of cold fury. Both shrews are mouse gray, with small black eyes nearly hidden by fur. Their eyesight is poor and they depend largely on a keen sense of smell to locate food. As a rule, neither species lives longer than two years.

The shrew's mission on earth is to eat: its metabolism is so rapid that it must consume its own weight in food every three or four hours. When all other sources of food fail, it turns to cannibalism. Fortunately, shrews are omnivorous, although they prefer live prey when they can catch it. They eat berries, nuts, grain, insects, earthworms, snails, salamanders, snakes, probably frogs, all types of mice and, no doubt, chipmunks. In addition to a formidable set of teeth and a ferocious disposition, the shrew's saliva contains a poison that slows a victim's heart and lung action, making it the only poisonous mammal in North America. The vole greatly outweighs the old field shrew, but hasn't a chance of surviving when it is caught in the open. Shrews are protected to some extent against predatory birds and mammals by a gland in each hind leg that releases a strong odor of musk, discouraging attacks. This may account for the dead but uneaten shrews often found on top of dikes, apparently dropped by hawks or owls.

On one occasion, when I was moving slowly and quietly along the border of a marsh, I heard a confused chorus of high-pitched squeaks. Peering between the tall marsh grasses, I saw two small shrews fighting. They rolled over and over in the soft snow, each attempting to get a firm hold on the other. Occasionally one would break loose and try to escape, but each time the other was on it in a flash.

Apparently, shrews are not harmed by their own venom, because neither appeared to let up. Finally, one maneuvered around until it grasped the other by the throat with its strong jaws. There was a spot of crimson on the white snow; the loser quivered a few times, then died. Wasting no time, the victor began to drag its meal into a burrow. I found myself marveling at the savagery of the encounter, and grateful that shrews don't grow to the size of grizzly bears.

A retired transportation engineer, **Louis W. Campbell** *was for many years the outdoor writer for the* Toledo Times *and is the author of* Birds of Lucas County *and* Birds of the Toledo Area. **Claire Gavin,** *a research associate at the University of Rochester, is his daughter.*

First Night of Summer in Chicago

ABE LOUISE YOUNG

I stayed awake all night listening to buses and trucks
go by till light blued the sky and a moth got in.
My cat caught the moth in his mouth but did not kill it.
He walked erect across the bedroom, tail high, teeth bared
while the moth fluttered hard against his palate,
buzzed and turned on the roof of his mouth.
He held it there, not biting down, till the flutter
almost subsided, then bent his head and opened
his mouth, let the moth fall out like a wet cherry pit
on my pillow, and come alive.

Abe Louise Young *lives in the Rogers Park neighborhood of Chicago. She teaches writing and reads poetry while enjoying all four seasons with her playful cat, Diego.*

A Flash of Gold

MARJORIE CARLSON DAVIS

Resourceful and resilient, coyotes are on the rebound, extending their range throughout the Great Lakes region. In this story, which takes place in Ontario, we see why some people distrust these crafty coyotes, and why others admire them greatly.

A coyote is a golden flash across the road, a flicker of movement in the brush, an eerie howl in the distance. Carly knows this. She also knows that to see—to really see—a coyote, a person must become as still as a tree, must tune her breathing to that of the wind.

Her brother Andrew taught her this. When they used to hike in the woods and meadows behind their house, Andrew showed her how to stop softly, quiet her breathing, and watch— a hummingbird at a flower, a loon floating on glassy water, a beaver gnawing on bark.

"You've got to be still, Carly," he told her. "You can't be crashing around or you'll scare the animals. Be quiet and listen."

Early one morning four years ago, when she was only nine, Carly and Andrew had spotted two coyotes at the meadow's edge. It was the first time she remembered seeing coyotes. Outlined by the rising sun, the animals looked tall, their legs long and bony, like wolves. Andrew caught Carly's arm, holding her silent until the coyotes vanished, evaporating into the morning mist.

"You know what reincarnation is?" Andrew asked.

Carly shook her head.

"It's a belief that you come back as something else, like an animal, after you die."

"That's spooky. Why'd you say that?"

"Because if reincarnation is true, that's what I want to return as, Carly." He nodded at the woods where the animals had disappeared. "I want to come back as a coyote."

"It still sounds weird," Carly said and paused, thinking. Then she added, "But why a coyote?"

Andrew gave a slight smile. "Because a coyote is smart and tricky, a great rebel against authority. He survives against all odds."

It is Saturday morning and Carly is at the Mini Mart, getting donuts while her mother waits in the car. Several farmers in overalls and dirty work boots stand by the coffee machine. One of them, Mr. McAlvoy, owns the land to the west of theirs, and Carly nods shyly at him as she picks out a cream pastry for her mother and a jelly-filled donut for herself. The farmers are talking about coyotes.

"This winter, Jim and I ran a pair down with our snowmobiles. Wore 'em out, then shot 'em," one of the men says, and they all nod.

"Cunning little devils, eh?" Mr. McAlvoy says. "Some stole the eggs right outta my hen house."

Carly smiles, silently cheering for the coyotes, those rebels, those tricky creatures. But her heart thumps when Mr. McAlvoy adds, "I've set some traps where they're getting in."

In the car on the way home, Carly eats her donut, sucking the jelly out of the center. She imagines she is a coyote sucking the yolk out of one of Mr. McAlvoy's eggs. Licking the sugar off her fingers, Carly thinks of the times she's truly seen coyotes, not the glimpses as they skulk along the back fence, or the bodies of dead ones along the road, but the moments when she's watched one in all its coyoteness. A mother with a ball of fluff in her jaws, carrying her pup to safety. One springing out of papery weeds to seize a mouse. Another with head cocked, peering curiously at its reflection in an early morning lake. She was always with Andrew when she saw them. Carly wonders if she will ever see one by herself, without Andrew's hand on her shoulder, his voice whispering "hush" in her ear.

As the car passes the curve overlooking Ice Lake, Carly holds her breath and turns her head away from the small white cross on the side of the road. She tries not to think of Andrew in his blue pickup, skidding on the ice, sailing off into partially frozen water. But she does anyway. She thinks of him every time they pass the cross.

Later that afternoon Carly tells her mother she's going for a walk, something she hasn't done for almost six months.

"Good, honey. I'm glad you're getting out," her mother says, and then, with a worried look, adds, "But stay away from the lake, okay? I don't want you out there by yourself."

It is early spring and still cold, but the snow has melted. Things will soon begin to turn green. The sun dodges in and out of clouds as Carly crosses the muddy field to the west, an expanse of churned brown earth and corn stubble. She doesn't plan to end up in Mr. McAlvoy's yard, but somehow there she is, scooting under his fence, darting over the still frozen clumps of grass, then circling his hen house.

Mr. McAlvoy has tried to cover the traps with tree branches and dead leaves, but Carly sees them, glinting. They look like big, steel dinosaur jaws.

"You put a stick in the center of them," she remembers Andrew telling her when they found traps out on their land. "Jiggle it around until the trap snaps."

Carly chooses her sticks, sturdy branches as thick as her arms. One. Two. Three. The traps spring easily, like snapping turtles. Crouching down like a thief, she hurries away, through the woods this time, to the meadow edging the lake.

In summer, the meadow buzzes with life. Insects hum and pop. Animals rustle through long grasses. But in fall, winter, and early spring, you have to look more closely to find life; Andrew taught her this, too.

The last time they came here was late fall. Andrew had challenged her to a game of hide and seek. One time he stayed hidden so long, she grew scared and then angry, at both Andrew's silence and the meadow's stillness. She yelled his name and stamped her feet until he came back, rushing at her from behind a tree, a streak of tan coat, a great weight as he toppled her.

"You weren't very quiet that time, Carly," he teased.

Now Carly looks at the woods, at the place where Andrew once disappeared and reappeared. Only darkness hovers behind the trees. All around her the meadow is silent, except for a faint whoosh of wind. Yellow brown grasses, trampled down by the winter's snows, seem empty.

The animals are here, only hiding; Carly can almost hear Andrew's voice. There are clues if you know where to look— deer pellets nesting in grass or raccoon prints in the mud.

Carly notices the wind growing stronger, sounding almost like a distant howl. The yellow grasses wave slightly as if something moves beneath them. Fear and anger rise in Carly, the way they did last fall when Andrew disappeared behind the trees. Tears wet her face. She pulls her arms close to her sides, holding herself still.

"Quiet. Listen. Watch," Andrew would have told her. She breathes in time to the wind and watches the bare tree branches, black scratches in the sky, stir gently. A crow rises from the woods with a squawk.

Andrew's not coming back this time, Carly knows. But somehow she feels that he is with her in a way she can't explain, in the things he has taught her, in her memories. She turns her head very slowly as if she knows the coyote will be there, even before she sees a flicker of movement emerging from the trees, a flash of gold in the sun.

Marjorie Carlson Davis, *whose favorite place is her summer home on Manitoulin Island, teaches writing at the college level and creative writing workshops for children for the Illinois Arts Council Arts in Literacy program. Her work has appeared in many publications, including* Many Mountains Moving, Indianapolis Monthly, *and the* Baltimore Review. *She has written two novels for adults and is finishing a middle-grade novel called* The Soda Pop Bear.

Beaver Rendezvous

ANN COOPER

Beavers played a major role in the exploration and settlement of the Great Lakes region. Prized for their pelts, which were turned into felt hats, beavers enticed fur trappers to the area and fueled a global fur trade that lasted more than two hundred years. Although their populations declined substantially because of this trade, beavers are now growing in number and once again are becoming a familiar sight on northern lakes.

We kept seeing their signs. They had littered the shoreline with peeled sticks, the ends pointed and tooth-marked. A floating branch of alder tangled in my paddle. The leaves were still green, but the bark looked chewed. We nosed our canoe into a tiny cove on the island. I stepped out into the shallows and yanked the canoe half onto shore so Jay could get out. We wanted to explore the island. But the going was rough—under and over. Birch, willow, and alder trees were strewn everywhere. Beavers had been *very* busy *very* recently. Now, at midday, the woods were quiet and still. The lake was calm and empty of wildlife. We knew we'd have to come back in the evening if we wanted to see beavers at work.

That evening, we put on long pants and long-sleeved shirts under our life jackets and lathered up with bug stuff, ready for our expedition. We felt like voyageurs.

The first good thing about going places by canoe is that it's silent—so silent you can glide along and not disturb wildlife. You can't shout or sing or talk loudly, of course. The second good thing is you can go in very shallow places. If you get stuck, you can back out. If you *really* get stuck, maybe caught halfway across an old beaver dam, you can get out and jiggle the canoe free—if you don't mind the idea of stepping into mud with leeches!

We paddled quietly, not talking except to share when we saw something neat: a mother merganser with a flotilla of fuzzy ducklings swimming through a reed-bed jungle; a green frog plopping off a lily leaf; two loons with black and white checkerboard backs and glossy heads that flip-dived and stayed under longer than I could hold my breath. I tried!

The trees on the island looked dark and shadowy, a bit spooky. We paddled splashlessly a canoe's length from land, listening with all our might. Sounds—the *whoo-who* of a distant owl, a twig cracking somewhere in the woods—sent shivers up my spine even though it was still fairly light. The beavers were nowhere to be seen.

Until . . . we rounded a rocky point and caught sight of a V-wake. Beaver! Only its head showed, a dark blob. I was so excited my paddle splashed. Instantly, we heard a sharp crack, saw a dark, glossy curve of black disappear underwater. The crack echoed. I couldn't believe a beaver's flat tail could splat such a loud alarm! I bet it warned every beaver for miles around that there were interlopers in beaver territory.

I once read that beavers used to come out by day. Now they are very wary. I suppose they were hunted for so long they learned to be super cautious. After all, hundreds of thousands of beavers were trapped for their soft, dense fur. Maybe millions for all I know. People made top hats out of the fur. That was a sick and cruel fashion. The voyageurs—that's travelers in French—were canoe experts, even on treacherous rapids. They paddled rivers and lakes and traded with Indians for beaver pelts and other animal skins. They sometimes paddled up to fourteen hours a day. Whew! And they could carry huge bundles of pelts, weighing about ninety pounds each, across portages. Portages are places where you carry your canoe from one lake or river to another, across often rocky or swampy land.

Each year the voyageurs gathered at a rendezvous—that's French for grand get-together. At the rendezvous they exchanged their bundles of beaver pelts for supplies and goods to trade for skins the next year.

Around the other side of the island we came to big reed beds where the bottom looked sandy-muddy. It was shallow. We got caught on an underwater log. I thought at first I'd have to get out and shove. Luckily, I used my paddle as a pushing pole and got us dislodged. Once through the weeds, we came to a narrow river. It wasn't a rapids kind of river, just glassy and slow. Both swampy banks grew sedges and low bushes. Beyond was forest. It looked like a place you'd see moose, but not this time. You could scarcely tell where land ended and river began, there were so many water lilies. They gleamed white in the dusk.

We paddled silently upstream until we came to a wide, lily-full place. There was no way through. But as I watched, something . . . a dark head . . . moved among the waterlilies. A lily leaf on a long stem waved and moved through the water. That was weird. We shipped our paddles, crouched low in our boat, and waited, straining our eyes to see in the gathering gloom.

The stem of the lily leaf got shorter and shorter. Finally the leaf blade disappeared. It had become a beaver's dinner. Funny, I thought they ate just bark. But this one kept grabbing chunks of lily and lily root. Bits were floating everywhere. Then it would swim over to the bank and mess about there, eating bits of branches. It held them in its front paws, turning the twigs as if they were corn on the cob. We were so close I could hear crunching.

I wish I could have stayed there all night, skulking in the canoe, watching beavers and listening to night quiet. But it was getting seriously dark. We had to get back to our cabin way across the lake.

I never really expected to rendezvous with beavers, let alone join their night-time party. Now I felt like a true voyageur of the north woods. We skimmed back around the shore as if powered by wings. The moon was a silvery face. A loon skittered, splashing along the water, and took off. As it flew it warbled its eerie cry. I yodeled back as best I could—a wild, warbling sound. I felt as if I were miles away in a different time in history—until I saw light in the cabin window and knew we were almost home.

❧

Ann Cooper, *past "Brit" and present ardent Coloradoan, is a teacher-on-the-trail and has written ten nature books for children. Her poetry and stories for children have appeared in several magazines, including* Spider, Ladybug, R-A-D-A-R, Friend, *and* Clubhouse.

Snowy Morning with Squirrels

RAYMOND SOUSTER

First Grey One
chasing Black One
(so fast the eye's weary
after thirty seconds of watching them),
along telephone wires
with a snow-layered insulation,
headlong down trees
dressed in ice-shiny bark,

then a little snow-hopping
for a change of pace,
and a final charge across the back fence
until they come together
for a moment's touching,

then it's Black One
chasing Grey One
up the nearest tree-trunk
(giving her a modest head-start),
and with my eyes still spinning
I watch the splendid game repeated
pole to ground to fence to tree,
wishing it could go on forever.

Raymond Souster *is one of Canada's best known poets. He is the author of many books of poetry, including many volumes of his* Collected Poems.

Gems in the Jack Pine

LAURIE ALLMANN

Less than five inches long, the Kirtland's warbler is a small but vital member of the Great Lakes community. For its survival, it depends on young jack pine forests, regular fires, and, now, the dedicated conservationists who are working to keep its habitat intact.

There is an island of sorts in the landlocked center of Michigan's Lower Peninsula. It is an island of cold air settled over the high plains of the Huron National Forest. At night the air runs down the slopes of the Maltby moraines and settles in the old glacial channels and lake basins. People here tell of how the killing frosts can come every month of the year. Right on through summer.

For the most part, it's not the kind of thing you notice on a July day. Hot still feels hot. But it makes itself known in the temperature averages and extremes, and in a shortening of the growing season. Translate these quiet circumstances to a plant, then add the bone-dry soils of grayling sand, and it becomes a shout, a riot, a howl. In the natural community, it is enough to make the difference between forest and barrens. Enough to keep out all the oaks except the northern pin oak, and to open the door for jack pine. Enough to delay the green-up of the grasses in spring, which historically meant one thing: fire—small, fast fires on a regular basis that would take out the understory and leave some mature trees alive, recording their passage as a charcoaled layer in the trees' annual rings. Every forty years or so there'd be a bigger, hotter fire that would take out all the trees and clear the way for a new forest like the one I see before me now.

It's called a "dog's hair" stand of jack pine, and it looks just like its name. The trees come up thick like this, small and plentiful, when the land is cleared and the jack pines are the first to lay claim to the exposed soil with the seeds of their fire-opened cones. The peer pressure of all their same-aged contemporaries keeps the trees small. The trees of this stand are fourteen years old, yet I could still encircle almost any given trunk with my two hands. Their heights all hover at about seven feet. They grow so close together that their branches interlace. It's not the kind of place that looks remotely inviting to walk through, which is just as well. It is better that no one walk there.

This forest has already been spoken for. Or, more accurately, it has already been sung for.

It belongs to the Kirtland's warbler. Not forever; just for ten years or so, when the jack pines are between about eight and about eighteen years of age; and within each year, only for the months of May through August, when the warblers breed. The rest of the year they are either in migration or are shifting and muttering through the scrubland of the Bahamas. Except for a few isolated sightings of migrants and apparently nonbreeding birds, that's it—the entire known scope of the species' limited range: the Bahamas, a handful of counties in Michigan where they nest, and the air in between.

The Kirtland's is among the rarest of birds on the planet. I don't mean that they are intrinsically more important than the Lincoln's sparrow whose song I hear at this moment, or than the ravens I saw earlier, hunched under the weight of their morning. Rareness speaks to the urgency of the call for action on our part. But considering the reach of the universe, any life is rare enough to turn my head.

At the time of this writing there are now thought to be 2,102 Kirtland's warblers drawing breath. That's 1,051 males counted while singing, and an inferred mate for each. At best it is an estimate, since some males have more than one mate and others are bachelors. Since people first began paying serious attention to their numbers, the census-estimated populations have sunk as low as 334 birds. Some attribute the low to the hurricane of 1973 that rampaged through their winter tropical territories, but a harder reason to face is the more likely one of habitat loss. A short-term boost in the bird's population, interestingly enough, is thought to have occurred in the aftermath of the first "big cut" of lumbering that came through middle America in the late 1800s. Although periodic openings had historically been created by natural fires, the extent of cleared land and mad slash fires that followed the big cut may have given rise to an unprecedented (albeit temporary) increase in the kind of dog's hair jack pine stands that the Kirtland's needs for nesting.

Their vulnerability is doled out in good measure: the parasitism of their nests by cowbirds who supplant the warbler eggs with their own, the dangers inherent in the long annual migration from which only 40 percent are thought to return, and a narrowly defined breeding habitat that is this ball suspended in the air, a community in perpetual adolescence. For when the trees grow high and large enough that their shade kills the plants below them, the warblers must move on to a place that gives better concealment to their ground nests. If such a place does not exist, then neither will the Kirtland's warbler.

I tell myself that it's fine if I don't see or hear one. After all, it's midsummer. The males have less reason to sing, and both the male and female have more reason to be secretive. Their territories require less work to defend. The nestlings of their first, and often only, brood of the season will already have fledged. If a second brood is under way, the female may be incubating eggs in her soft nest of grass and deer hair, hidden beneath the prairie grasses and blueberries. In any case, they have better things to do than be seen.

From this vantage along a national forest road (it is illegal to enter the forest during the breeding season, since the Kirtland's is federally listed as an endangered species), I train my binoculars on the jack pine cones clinging to the tips of the trees. In the poetry of adaptation, the warblers' fledglings are said to resemble nothing so much as the cone of a jack pine. I see only pine cones. That is, as far as I can tell. Among them may be a great impersonation of a pine cone.

The allure of rare animals can blind you to what is around them. Everything in the vicinity is measured as good or bad relative to its known influence on the creature whose population is in trouble. The result is a skewed and partial vision of what is a much more complex system made not only of the known, but more important, of the *unknown,* elements that make it work.

This particular stand of jack pines is here, not from fire, but because it was planted with the sole intent of creating warbler habitat that had diminished because of our modern habit of putting out the fires that lightning starts. Fortunately, these managed stands of jack pine have proved to be acceptable breeding sites for the Kirtland's. But those who stand, as I do today, in hopes of seeing one of "the 2,102," are in the midst of more than the Kirtland's summer range. Beyond this manmade dog's hair stand with its precious dwellers is the larger community within which it exists.

Before the era of forests as crops, this part of Michigan was a blend of dry sand prairie and pine barrens. It was not the solid green curtain of forest that many have now come to consider synonymous with natural beauty. It had its own brand of beauty, a stark and wind-whittled eloquence expressed not only in trees, but also in bluestem and rice grass, Indian grass, the yellow flowers of the pale agoseris, the bright green fans of rough fescue grass, and the Hill's thistle that would spend four years preparing for its one white blossom. With them were the animals of open country: the vesper sparrow, the clay-colored sparrow, the hog-nosed snake, the coyote, the badger.

Apart from management for the Kirtland's warbler, work is also under way at the Huron National Forest to clear some tracts of land to allow this other rare element to survive: in a word, the element of "openness." Each season following a clearing reveals more and more of the historic native plants trying to recolonize after two hundred years of suppression, reveling in the so-called poor soils that, for them, are the soils of home.

The song is clear and loud. I see the male with his gray back and yellow breast. His body shakes with the effort of every note. The labels and numbers fall away. I can tell in a glance that he does not know he is endangered. He knows only that his job is to sing, this day, from the top of that young jack pine. His beak is open, full of the sky behind him.

Laurie Allmann *writes essays and poetry from her home in the St. Croix River Valley of Minnesota. She is the author of* Far from Tame: Landscapes at the Heart of a Continent, *from which this essay is taken. Allmann has been a featured commentator on Minnesota Public Radio, and has adapted natural history essays for live performance. Her recent writing has focused on script development for a series of environmental documentary films. She has worked as a wilderness canoe guide and naturalist.*

Appendixes

Ecology of the
Great Lakes

What Is an Ecoregion?

The *Stories from Where We Live* series celebrates the literature of North America's diverse ecoregions. Ecoregions are large geographic areas that share similar climate, soils, and plant and animal communities. Thinking ecoregionally helps us understand how neighboring cities and states are connected, and makes it easier to coordinate the use and protection of shared rivers, forests, watersheds, mountain ranges, and other natural areas. We believe that ecoregions also provide an illuminating way to organize and compare place-based literature.

While many institutions have mapped the world's ecoregions, no existing delineation of ecoregions (or similar unit, such as *provinces* or *bioregions*) proved perfectly suited to a literary series. We created our own set of ecoregions based largely on existing scientific designations, with an added consideration for regional differences in human culture.

NORTHWEST
PACIFIC
COAST

THI

BOREA

GREAT

NORT

ROCKY MOUNTAINS

CALIFORNIA
COAST

WESTERN
DESERTS
AND
PLATEAUS

HAWAIIAN
ISLANDS

ARCTIC

FOREST

AMERICAN

PRAIRIE

GREAT LAKES

NORTHEAST WOODLANDS

NORTH ATLANTIC COAST

APPALACHIAN HIGHLANDS

SOUTHERN HILL COUNTRY

SOUTH ATLANTIC COAST AND PIEDMONT

GULF COAST

Defining the Great Lakes

If you were an astronaut circling Earth, few North American features would stand out more clearly to you than the Great Lakes. These five water bodies contain one-fifth of all the world's freshwater. They are large enough to make their own weather, and drain an area of land, known as their *watershed,* that is more than 200,000 square miles.

For these and many other reasons, we chose to recognize the Great Lakes as one of the ecoregions in this series. Our ecoregion is roughly comparable to the Great Lakes watershed. Its boundaries trace a broad outline around the five Great Lakes, encompassing parts of Minnesota, Wisconsin, Illinois, Indiana, Ohio, Pennsylvania, New York, and Ontario, as well as both peninsulas of Michigan.

The Great Lakes themselves occupy nearly a third of this ecoregion. *Lake Superior* is the wildest and largest of the group—so large that you could pour the other four lakes into its basin and it would still not overflow. In fact, Superior is the largest freshwater lake in the world. *Lake Michigan* is second in size, providing an oceanlike wilderness to Milwaukee, Chicago, and other cities that lie beside it. Lake Superior flows directly into *Lake Huron* via the St. Mary's River. Forests and farms surround Lake Huron in the north and south, respectively. *Lake Erie,* the shallowest and warmest Great Lake, is also the most dangerous because of the fierce west-east winds that roar across it. It spills directly into *Lake Ontario* through the narrow Niagara River. Lake Ontario, the smallest Great Lake, borders major cities to the west, and towns and farms in most of the rest of its range.

All five Great Lakes, and the lands around them, were shaped by the glaciers that scoured the region more than 14,000 years ago. As these glaciers advanced, they distributed rich soils across the area, creating fertile ground for wild plants and, later, crops. On their retreat, the glaciers left hills and ridges in their wake, as well as basins and holes that filled with meltwater to form the region's many lakes. More than 10,000 glacial lakes dot the lands along the Wisconsin-Michigan border alone.

Today the five Great Lakes exert a powerful influence over the entire region. Over the course of the summer, their water temperature increases, storing up energy that is released later in the fall when temperatures descend. The result is the so-called "lake-effect"—winds and moisture that produce clouds and rainfall in the autumn and help create the snowbelt that blankets the southern and eastern sides of the lakes during the winter months. The lakes also help moderate temperatures. Summers are cooler and winters warmer in many parts of the Great Lakes basin than in other places at similar latitudes.

The lakes influence the region's plant and animal life in many ways. Not only do they support abundant fish and mollusks, but their surrounding dunes, marshes, and swamps nurture many wild species. Despite the dominating presence of the five Great Lakes, though, the ecoregion as a whole should not be thought of exclusively in terms of its freshwater resources. Tallgrass prairies, oak savannas, hardwood forests, and many other habitats diversify the landscape and provide a mix of living spaces for wild creatures.

For thousands of years, Potawatomi, Ojibwe, Menominee, Iroquois, Miami, Shawnee, and other native groups inhabited the Great Lakes region, surviving on ample stocks of fish, berries, mammals, wild rice, and other natural resources. In the 1600s, French explorers, or *voyageurs*, journeyed across the Great Lakes, lured by the seemingly endless quantities of beavers and other mammals whose furs were in high demand throughout Europe. Setting up travel routes, learning native languages, and building trading forts, these early trappers paved the way for later generations of settlers who came to the region for its bountiful natural resources. Timber, ores, fish, and productive farmland all attracted new inhabitants over the years. Some of the largest communities in the region grew up on the banks of the Great Lakes, at convenient sites from which to travel and transport goods into and out of the area.

If you look at a map of the Great Lakes region today, you'll notice that its largest cities are still perched right on the edge of the Great Lakes themselves. Time, however, has brought many changes to the region, not all of them welcome. Pollution, overfishing, suburban growth, and the spread of invasive species such as zebra mussels and purple loosestrife have all played a role in declining environmental quality. But the people who live around the Great Lakes have demonstrated a growing commitment to restore and sustain their treasured local resources, including the vast lakes themselves, for generations to come.

Habitats

The diversity of the Great Lakes is unusually high. Not only do the lakes create many rich coastal environments, but the region as a whole over-lies parts of three major terrestrial communities: the boreal forest to the north, the deciduous woodlands to the east, and the tallgrass prairie to the west. Contained within the region, then, are a wealth of wildlife habitats—places that provide animals with the food, shelter, space, and living conditions they need to survive. The descriptions below highlight some of the most important of these Great Lakes habitats.

Lakes: From enormous Lake Superior to tiny interior lakes just a few hundred yards across, freshwater lakes are a trademark of the Great Lakes region. The definition of a lake is a water body deep enough that sunlight does not reach some part of the lake bottom. Hundreds of thousands of these lakes were carved out of the landscape by the great earth-moving glaciers of the last Ice Age. And many others have been created by a single diligent mammal: the beaver!

Row across any lake and you'll notice a pattern to the distribution of life: many more organisms fill the sunlit edges than the open water. In the middle of a small inland lake, for example, you might spot only an occasional teal or merganser on the water. Northern pike swim just below the surface, while bass and walleye channel through the cold depths. Head toward shore, though, and the wildlife viewing picks up, especially where the lake becomes shallow enough to support plant life. Mallards with young ducklings paddle close to the land's edge, ready to jump out for shelter or a quick insect snack. Red-winged blackbirds, muskrats, and wading birds congregate in the cattails and reeds where prey such as insects and small fish abound. Even deer, moose, and other land animals visit the outer margins of the water to drink and feast on aquatic plants. All of these creatures and more are bound together in a freshwater food web that begins with the tiniest plankton and aquatic plants and continues up through small fish and invertebrates to top predators such as northern pike and bass, to the very top predators: great blue herons, eagles, and humans. (Examples: "Chicago Waters"; "The Ice Deer"; "At Uglyfish Lake"; "Saving Lake Erie"; "The Glowing Brown Snails of Blueberry Lake"; "Great Northern Pike.")

Dunes: In some parts of the Great Lakes, broad sandy beaches stretch along the water's edge, providing comfortable footing for sunbathers and beachcombers. Even more spectacular are the rounded sand dunes that rise as high as four hundred feet above the water in some parts of the region. Some of the most stellar freshwater sand dunes in the world lie within the Great Lakes region, most notably along the Lake Michigan

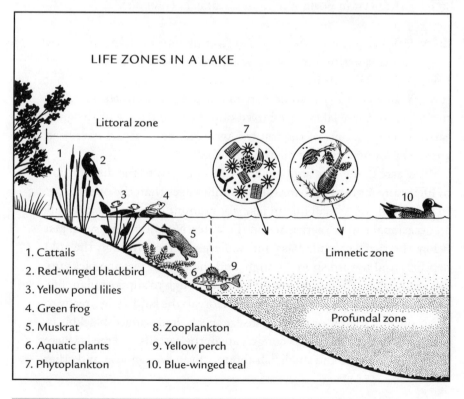

LIFE ZONES IN A LAKE

Littoral zone

Limnetic zone

Profundal zone

1. Cattails
2. Red-winged blackbird
3. Yellow pond lilies
4. Green frog
5. Muskrat
6. Aquatic plants
7. Phytoplankton
8. Zooplankton
9. Yellow perch
10. Blue-winged teal

shoreline in Indiana and Michigan. In general, sand dunes are not known for supporting a whole lot of plant or animal life. Their conditions are simply too dry, hot, and low in nutrients. Nonetheless, the sand dunes and nearby barrens of the Great Lakes are among the ecologically most important habitats of the region. That's because they house many forms of life found nowhere else on Earth, including the dune thistle, Houghton's goldenrod, and the Lake Huron locust. (Examples: "We Are the Early Risers"; "Fireworks!")

Rivers and Streams: Rivers and streams are the arteries of the Great Lakes landscape, carrying everything good and bad alike from one part of the region to another. In many areas, they're the last remaining undeveloped corridors, giving wild animals a sheltered path between different habitats. In addition, rivers transport nutrients, such as those stored in the annual autumn leaf fall, from upland to downstream habitats. Unfortunately,

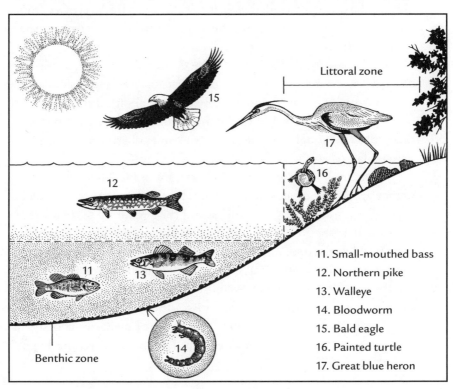

11. Small-mouthed bass
12. Northern pike
13. Walleye
14. Bloodworm
15. Bald eagle
16. Painted turtle
17. Great blue heron

they also carry silt and pollutants generated by human activities to places farther downstream, including the Great Lakes themselves.

You'll find many species common to lakes inhabiting the region's rivers, including frogs, turtles, ducks, wading birds, and beavers. If you're lucky, you might catch sight of a river otter sliding down a slick streambank, or see a raccoon catching crayfish under the moonlight. Kingfishers, swallows, salamanders, and minks are just a few of the many other creatures that rely on rivers throughout this region. (Examples: "Adrift on Niagara"; "Milwaukee River Poem"; "Serious Fishing"; "The Turtle.")

Marshes: Venture into a cattail marsh on a typical summer day, and you'll feel like you've just stepped into a concert hall filled with many strange instruments. You'll hear the *konkaree* of red-winged blackbirds, the whine of mosquitoes, and the deep bass thrumming of bullfrogs. During the spring and fall, these sounds can reach the level of a cacophony as thousands of migrating birds pause to rest on their journeys north and south.

Marshes are found throughout the Great Lakes region, at the edge of lakes, on the margins of rivers, or in wet, shallow depressions in the terrain. You can often recognize them by the tall cattail stalks that rise in the air, waving their brown seedheads like a conductor's baton. In many places, though, purple loosestrife and other non-native plants have replaced cattails as the dominant vegetation.

Wherever marshes grow, they attract a lot of life. Mosquitoes, dragonflies, frogs, and other small creatures breed in the standing water between the grasses. Many fish, too, spend the beginning of their lives in these sheltered, nutrient-rich waters. Muskrats and other small mammals build their nests under the reeds, feasting on steady supplies of cattails and other plants. Tall wading birds, such as herons and cranes, ply the water for invertebrates and fish. And many marshes, such as those along southern Lake Erie and southern Lake Michigan, are a breeding and resting ground for great flocks of mallards, coots, rails, and other resident and migrating birds. (Examples: "Evening Flight"; "Shorthand on the Snow.")

Swamps and Bogs: The words "marsh," "swamp," and "bog" are often used interchangeably, but each of these places is a distinct wetland habitat. Marshes always have lots of standing water and are dominated by grasslike plants. Swamps are not as wet as marshes, and often support trees such as red maples and alders. Black bears, snowshoe hares, and moose share swamp habitat with a variety of birds, reptiles, and amphibians. Bogs are wet, spongy areas that form where water enters and doesn't stir. Over time, decaying plant matter forms a mat across the water that's thick enough to walk on. But unlike marshes and swamps, bog are low in nutrients. In fact, the soils are so acidic that only a few highly adapted species such as pitcher plants and sphagnum mosses can grow there. Still, four-toed salamanders, meadow voles, and short-eared owls are among the many animals that find food and shelter in bogs and bog forests. (Examples: "The Gold Medal Flower"; "An Evening on Isle Royale"; "Beaver Rendezvous.")

Grassy Fields: The first Europeans who ventured westward into the heart of America reported the thrill of emerging from the shadows of the eastern forests into broad, open grasslands bathed in sunlight. Today, open fields continue to be relished by both people and wildlife. Groggy woodchucks, emerging from hibernation, can be found basking on the warmed-up ground, the first areas to lose their snowpack each spring. Mice, voles, shrews, and rabbits zig-zag through the grasses year-round, nibbling on plants and other foods. Hawks circle overhead, keen on spotting one of these small mammals in the exposed terrain.

If you find an open grassy area in the Great Lakes region, it may be the same sort of habitat those early Europeans encountered: a tiny piece of the tallgrass prairie. These prairie patches were once found in many parts of Illinois, Indiana, southern Michigan, and Ohio, and a few have been preserved. Other wild grassy habitats in the region are oak savannas (common in Illinois), meadows, and even untamed hay fields. The common denominator in all these places is the persistence of grass instead of forest. Fire, animal grazing, and thick root systems all play a role in keeping the grass in and the trees out. And when that happens, you can be sure that bobolinks, butterflies, meadowlarks, and myriad small mammals will enjoy these fertile open spaces. (Examples: "Fairies' Washing"; "Prairie after Rain"; "Hay Field Bestiary.")

Hardwood Forests: Take a walk through a hardwood forest in the Great Lakes region and you'll see many signs of life. Crows gather in the tree-tops, keeping a sharp eye on the activity below. Squirrels leap from branch to branch as they try to reach the most elusive acorns. Red-headed woodpeckers jab at the tree trunks, searching for the many insects burrowed in the bark. Beneath the trees, chipmunks scramble over roots and logs, and snakes slither through the soggy leaf litter.

You'll find a variety of hardwood forests in the Great Lakes region. In the southern part of the region, oaks, hickories, maples, and beech trees grow in the rich soil. In the colder northern parts, aspens and birches grow interspersed with conifers such as pines and spruces. Along the edges of rivers, willows and alder hold fast to the wet stream-banks. Common to all these hardwood forests is an abundance of plant and animal life, as well as a spectacular show of leafy color as the chill of autumn settles in. (Examples: "A Mighty Fortress"; "The Box Camera.")

Conifer Forests: If you had been alive in the early 1800s, you could have walked through some of the most extraordinary forests that have ever graced this country: the vast white and red pine forests of New York and Pennsylvania, northern Michigan, Wisconsin, and Minnesota. According to some accounts, white pines towered more than two hundred feet over the open, needle-covered forest floor. To some people, walking in these great pine forests felt like standing in a hushed and awesome cathedral.

Sadly, most of the original red and white pine forest was toppled in a great wave of timbercutting that spread westward in the mid- to late-nineteenth century. But you can still find remnants of it in a few parts of the Great Lakes, and still find other needle-leafed forests throughout the region. Jack pines sprouted up where white and red pines had been cut and burned. Spruce and fir forests, the great boreal forests of the far north, reach down into some of the most northerly parts of the Great Lakes region. And you'll also find pine trees growing in gaps in the hardwood forests, quick to colonize open ground with their light-weight, sun-loving seeds.

Conifer trees get their name from the seed-bearing cones that fill their branches. Nuthatches and other birds hop along the tree trunks, plucking these seeds out for a quick, nutritious meal. Chipmunks and mice eat them on the ground. Spruce grouse nibble the twigs of conifer trees, and porcupines gnaw on their inner bark. Conifer forests provide shelter for many species, including moose, snowshoe hares, and white-tailed deer, especially during winter snowfall. And one particular kind of conifer forest—young stands of jack pines—are the one and only habitat for the very rare Kirtland's warbler. (Examples: "Moon Magic"; "Return Portage"; "Neengay, the Story Giver"; "A Bear in the Backyard"; "Gems in the Jack Pine.")

Cities and Suburbs: Walking through a city or town in the Great Lakes region, you can find many animal species that have adapted to the frag-mentation of wild habitat and the presence of so many people. Rac-coons nest in street trees and telephone poles, and forage in garbage cans instead of forests. Hawks find a quick meal among the overfed pi-geons that flock in local parks. Squirrels, mice, skunks, and opossums eat discarded food, and find adequate shelter in backyard trees and scattered woodlands.

One notable characteristic of urbanized areas is the preponderance of plants and animals imported from other regions. Norway maples, European beeches, cherry trees, purple loosestrife, gypsy moths, and starlings are among the many species that have come to the Great Lakes region from other countries. In some cases, these species are a welcome addition to the urban landscape. In other cases, however, scientists are trying to control the invader to restore territory to less aggressive native species, such as cattails, woodpeckers, and bluebirds. (Examples: "The Copper Beech"; "Leaves"; "The Raccoon Brigade"; "Four Skinny Trees"; "First Night of Summer in Chicago.")

Animals and Plants

Spend time exploring the varied habitats of the Great Lakes region, and you'll be able to find hundreds of species of birds, mammals, fish, and more. In this list, we've recorded those species that are mentioned in the literature of this anthology.

Birds: The Great Lakes region attracts many *ducklike birds,* including loons, mergansers, mallards, teals, and Canada geese. Herring gulls, sometimes called seagulls, are known as *aerialists.* Great blue herons are some of the *long-legged wading birds* of the region. *Birds of prey* found here include eagles, red-tailed hawks, Cooper's hawks, and barred owls and other owls. Wild turkeys, ruffed grouse, and ring-necked pheasants are all *fowl-like birds.* Mourning doves, ruby-throated hummingbirds, and pileated woodpeckers are classified as *nonperching land birds.* And the *perching birds* of the region include meadow-larks, ravens, bobolinks, crows, red-winged black-birds, horned larks, savannah sparrows, song sparrows, tree sparrows, Lincoln's sparrows, vesper sparrows, clay-colored sparrows, swallows, chick-adees, prothonotary warblers, Kirtland's warblers, starlings, juncos, cardinals, blue jays, marsh wrens and other wrens, goldfinches, pine siskins, redpolls, cedar waxwings, and cowbirds.

Hooded Mergansers

Red-Winged Blackbird

Mammals: Among the many large mammals of the Great Lakes are moose, white-tailed deer, black bears, coyotes, and wolves. Small to medium-sized mammals include deer mice, white-footed mice, meadow mice or voles, short-tailed shrews, field shrews, chipmunks, fox squirrels, gray squirrels, black squirrels, bats, cottontail rabbits, snowshoe hares, muskrats, weasels, minks, skunks, opossums, raccoons, woodchucks, badgers, otters, and beavers.

Muskrat

Invertebrates: Many *insects* crawl, hop, and flit about the Great Lakes region, including ants, beetles, ladybugs, praying mantises, grasshoppers, mosquitoes, hornets, bumblebees, dragonflies, butterflies, and moths. Other invertebrates of the region include earthworms, spiders, leeches, and snails.

Hornet

Reptiles and Amphibians: Snapping turtles and other turtles make up a large group of Great Lakes *reptiles,* as do black rat snakes, garter snakes, hog-nosed snakes, and other snakes. The region's *amphibians* include many kinds of frogs and salamanders.

Snapping Turtle

Fish: Freshwater fish abound in the Great Lakes themselves and in surrounding lakes, rivers, and streams. Among these fish are alewives, northern pike, whitefish, walleyes, bass, carp, channel catfish, crappies, muskies or muskellunge, minnows, perch, German Browns or brown trout, and other trout.

Brown Trout

Plants: Trees and shrubs of the region include *conifers* such as white pines and jack pines, balsam firs, hemlock, cedars, junipers, and spruces. Among the region's *broadleaf trees and shrubs* are oaks, birches, dogwood, basswood, poplar, maples, mountain ash, hawthorn, apple trees, cherry trees, willows, alder, leatherleaf, sumac, forsythia, redbuds, blueberries, blackberries, and raspberries. *Wildflowers and grasses* of the region include ragweed, asters, marigolds, chicory, boneset, dandelion, sunflowers, black-eyed Susans, goldenrod, Queen Anne's lace, cattails, bluestem, trillium, rice grass, Indian grass, sedges, pale agoseris, fescue grass, Hill's thistle, evening primrose, fringed gentians, wild grapes, wild rice, tiger lilies, milkweed, wild mint, cockleburs, bindweed, yellow lady's slipper, wild strawberry, and water lilies. *Ferns* are in their own plant group.

Fringed Gentian

Other: Mushrooms and oyster-shell scale are two kinds of *fungi*. Neither fungi nor the group of organisms known as *algae* are now considered part of the plant family.

Stories by State or Province

Illinois

1. "Chicago Waters" (Chicago)
2. "A Clutch of Flowers" (Kankakee County)
3. "Prairie after Rain" (Lake Forest)
4. "Christmas Tree Miracle" (Chicago) *(also Michigan)*
5. "Four Skinny Trees" (Chicago)
6. "Crows" (Naperville)
7. "First Night of Summer in Chicago" (Chicago)

Indiana

8. "Fairies' Washing" (North Liberty)
9. "The Gold Medal Flower" (Rome City)
10. "The Box Camera" (near Valparaiso)

Michigan

11. "The Ice Deer" (Wayne County)
12. "From the Cellar" (East Lansing)
13. "Winter Season" (Benzonia)
14. "Fireworks!" (Frankfort area)
15. "At Uglyfish Lake" (Newberry)
16. "Mush Again" (the Downriver Area)
17. "Leaves" (Ann Arbor)
4. "Christmas Tree Miracle" (Thompson) *(also Illinois)*
18. "Journal Entry: Lake Michigan, July" (Whitehall)
19. "Serious Fishing" (Ann Arbor and Ypsilanti)
20. "Great Northern Pike" (Honor)

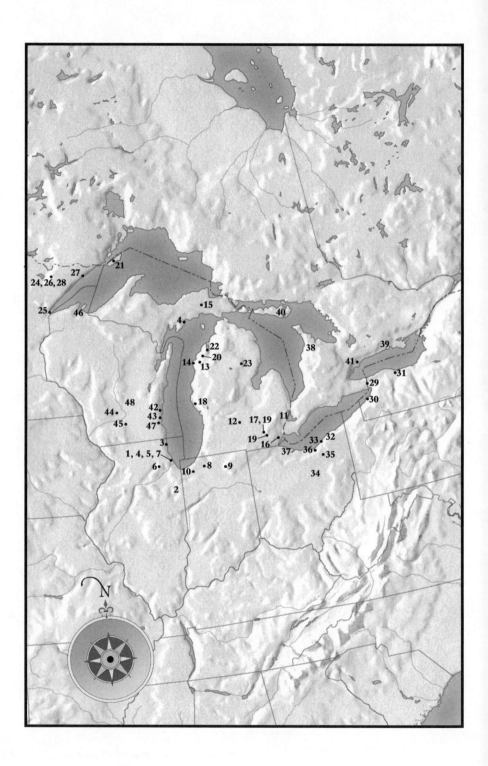

21. "An Evening on Isle Royale" (Isle Royale)
22. "Hummingbird" (Traverse City)
23. "Gems in the Jack Pine" (Huron National Forest)

Minnesota

24. "Moon Magic" (Ely)
25. "Return Portage" (Duluth)
26. "The Glowing Brown Snails of Blueberry Lake" (Ely)
27. "A Bear in the Backyard" (Grand Marais)
28. "Beaver Rendezvous" (near Ely)

New York

29. "Adrift on Niagara" (Niagara Falls) *(also Ontario)*
30. "Saving Lake Erie" (Dunkirk)
31. "The Copper Beech" (Rochester)

Ohio

32. "Miracle" (Lake County)
33. "Evening Flight" (Mentor-on-the-Lake)
34. "Hay Field Bestiary" (Holmes County)
35. "Summer at Silver Creek Farm" (Hiram)
36. "Rain" (Cleveland)
37. "Shorthand on the Snow" (southwestern Lake Erie marshes)

Ontario

29. "Adrift on Niagara" (Niagara Falls) *(also New York)*
38. "The Worm Girl" (Grey Bruce Counties)
39. "Apple Jelly" (southern Ontario)
40. "A Flash of Gold" (Manitoulin Island)
41. "Snowy Morning with Squirrels" (Toronto)

Wisconsin

42. "We Are the Early Risers" (Shorewood)

Parks and Preserves

Listed below are just a few of the many places where you can go to experience the wilder side of the Great Lakes ecoregion. Bear in mind that although all of these states and provinces, with the exception of Michigan, straddle more than one ecoregion, we have included only parks and preserves that lie in their Great Lakes portions. Also, please note that the phone numbers provided sometimes are for the park's headquarters, but often are for a managing agency or organization. In any case, the people at these numbers can provide you with details about the area and directions for how to get there.

Illinois

Barbara Key Park (Lake in the Hills) 815-669-4100
Black Partridge Woods (River Forest) 708-771-1330
Bluff Spring Fen Nature Preserve (Chicago) 312-580-2100
Braidwood Dunes and Savanna Nature Preserve (Joliet) 815-727-8700
Chain O'Lakes State Park (Spring Grove) 847-587-5512
Goose Lake Prairie State Natural Area (Morris) 815-942-2899
Grant Creek Prairie Nature Preserve (Wilmington) 815-423-5326
Harlem Hills Nature Preserve (Loves Park) 815-885-3612
Illinois Beach State Park (Zion) 847-662-4811
Kankakee River State Park (Bourbonnais) 815-933-1383
Middle Fork Woods Nature Preserve (Oakwood) 217-442-4915
Momence Wetlands Nature Preserve (Beaverville) 815-933-1383
Morton Arboretum (Lisle) 630-968-0074
Ryerson Woods (Deerfield) 847-968-3321
Upper Embarras Woods Nature Preserve (Charleston) 217-346-3360
Volo Bog State Natural Area (Ingleside) 815-344-1294

Indiana

Chain O'Lakes State Park (Albion) 260-636-2654

Crooked Lake Nature Preserve (Fort Wayne) 317-232-4052

Fox Island Nature Preserve (Fort Wayne) 219-627-3289

Gibson Woods Nature Preserve (Crown Point) 219-844-3188

Hoosier Prairie Nature Preserve (Indianapolis) 317-232-4080

Indiana Dunes National Lakeshore (Porter) 219-926-7561, ext. 225

Indiana Dunes State Park (Chesterton) 219-926-1952

Jasper-Pulaski Fish and Wildlife Area (Medaryville) 219-843-4841

Pine Hills Nature Preserve (Waveland) 765-435-2810

Portland Arch Nature Preserve (Indianapolis) 317-232-4080

Potato Creek State Park (North Liberty) 574-656-8186

Potawatomi Nature Preserve (Angola) 317-232-4052

Rocky Hollow Nature Preserve (Marshall) 317-232-4052

Salamonie River State Forest (Lagro) 219-782-2349

Tamarack Bog Nature Preserve (Mongo) 219-367-2164

Tefft Savanna Nature Preserve (Indianapolis) 219-843-4841

Willow Slough State Fish and Wildlife Area (Morocco)
219-285-2704

Michigan

Algonac State Park (Marine City) 810-765-5605

Estivant Pines Sanctuary (Avoca) 800-338-7982

Grass River Natural Area (Bellaire) 231-533-8314

Hartwick Pines State Park (Grayling) 517-348-2537

Hiawatha National Forest (Escanaba) 906-786-4062

Isle Royale National Park (Houghton) 906-482-0984

Ludington State Park (Ludington) 231-843-8671

Nordhouse Dunes Wilderness Area (Cadillac) 800-821-6263

Pictured Rocks National Lakeshore (Munising) 906-387-3700

Porcupine Mountains Wilderness State Park (Ontonagon)
906-885-5275

Seney National Wildlife Refuge (Seney) 906-586-9851

Shiawassee National Wildlife Refuge (Saginaw) 989-777-5930

Skegemog Swamp Wildlife Area (Lansing) 517-373-1275
Sleeping Bear Dunes National Lakeshore (Empire) 231-326-5134
Sylvania Wilderness (Watersmeet) 906-358-4551
Tawas Point State Park (East Tawas) 517-362-5041
Tobico Marsh (Bay City) 517-667-0717
Warren Dunes State Park (Sawyer) 616-426-4013
Waterloo State Recreation Area (Chelsea) 734-475-8307
Whitefish Point Bird Observatory (Paradise) 906-492-3596

Minnesota

Bear Head Lake State Park (Ely) 218-365-7229
Boundary Waters Canoe Area (Ely area) 877-550-6777
Cascade River State Park (Lutsen) 218-387-3053
George H. Crosby Manitou State Park (Finland) 218-226-6365
Gooseberry Falls State Park (Two Harbors) 218-834-3855
Jay Cooke State Park (Carlton) 218-384-4610
Judge C. R. Magney State Park (Grand Marais) 218-387-3039
Moose Lake State Park (Moose Lake) 218-485-5420
Rice Lake National Wildlife Refuge (McGregor) 218-768-2402
Superior National Forest (Duluth) 218-626-4300
Temperance River State Park (Schroeder) 218-663-7476
Tettegouche State Park (Silver Bay) 218-226-6365

New York

Allegany State Park (Salamanca) 716-354-9121
Evangola State Park (Irving) 716-549-1802
Golden Hill State Park (Barker) 716-795-3885
Iroquois National Wildlife Refuge (Basom) 585-948-5445
Island Parks (Clayton) 315-654-2522
Lake Erie State Park (Brockton) 716-792-9124
Montezuma National Wildlife Refuge (Seneca Falls) 315-568-5987
Old Erie Canal State Park (Kirkville) 315-687-7821
Southwick Beach State Park (Woodville) 315-846-5338
Wellesley Island State Park (Fineview) 315-482-2722

Ohio

Bedford Reservation (Cleveland) 216-351-6300
Cedar Point National Wildlife Refuge (Oak Harbor) 419-898-0014
Crane Creek State Park (Oregon) 419-836-7758
Cuyahoga Valley National Park (Brecksville) 216-524-1497
Fowler Woods State Nature Preserve (Tiffin) 614-265-6453
Goll Woods State Nature Preserve (Archbold) 419-445-1775
Headlands Dunes State Nature Preserve (Columbus) 216-881-8141
Irwin Prairie State Nature Preserve (Archbold) 419-445-1775
Mohican State Park (Loudinville) 419-994-4290
North Chagrin Reservation (Cleveland) 216-351-6300
Oak Openings Metropark (Toledo) 419-535-3058
Ottawa National Wildlife Refuge (Oak Harbor) 419-898-0014
Sheldon Marsh State Nature Preserve (Huron) 419-433-4601
Springville Marsh State Nature Preserve (Tiffin) 614-265-6453
Wildcat Hollow (Athens) 740-753-0101

Ontario

Algonquin Provincial Park (Whitney) 705-633-5572
Bruce Peninsula National Park (Tobermory) 519-596-2233
Earl Rowe Provincial Park (Alliston) 705-435-2498
Emily Provincial Park (Omemee) 705-799-5170
Killarney Provincial Park (Killarney) 705-857-3228
Lake Superior Provincial Park (Wawa) 705-856-2284
MacGregor Point Provincial Park (Port Elgin) 519-389-9056
Point Pelee National Park (Leamington) 519-322-2365
Port Burwell Provincial Park (Port Burwell) 519-874-4691
White Lake Provincial Park (White Lake) 807-822-2447

Pennsylvania

Allegheny National Forest (Warren) 814-723-5150
Presque Isle State Park (Erie) 814-833-7424
Pymatuning State Park (Jamestown) 724-932-3141

Wisconsin

Amnicon Falls State Park (Superior) 715-398-3000

Apostle Islands National Lakeshore (Bayfield) 715-779-3397

Chequamegon National Forest (Park Falls) 715-762-2461

Chiwaukee Prairie State Natural Area (Pleasant Prairie) 262-884-2391

Copper Falls State Park (Mellen) 715-274-5123

Crex Meadows Wildlife Area (Grantsburg) 715-463-2896

Dunbar Barrens State Natural Area (Marinette) 715-732-5511

Flambeau River State Forest (Winter) 715-332-5271

Horicon National Wildlife Refuge (Mayville) 920-387-2658

Ice Age National Scenic Trail (Madison) 608-441-5615

Kettle Moraine State Forest—Northern Unit (Campbellsport)
    262-626-2116

Kettle Moraine State Forest—Southern Unit (Eagle) 262-594-6200

Kohler Dunes Natural Area (Sheboygan) 920-451-4080

Lulu Lake State Natural Area (Eagle) 262-642-7276

Lynch Creek Waterfowl Area (Hayward) 715-634-4821

Recommended Reading

William Ashworth. *The Late, Great Lakes: An Environmental History*. New York: Alfred A. Knopf, 1986.

Burton Verne Barnes. *Michigan Trees: A Guide to the Trees of Michigan and the Great Lakes States*. Ann Arbor, Mich.: University of Michigan Press, 1981.

James H. Harding. *Amphibians of the Great Lakes Region*. Ann Arbor, Mich.: University of Michigan Press, 1997.

Sharon Katz. *The Great Lakes (Ecosystems of North America)*. Tarrytown, N.Y.: Marshall Cavendish Corp., 1998.

Peggy Kochanoff. *A Field Guide to Nearby Nature: Fields and Woods of the Midwest and East Coast.* Missoula, Mont.: Mountain Press Publishing Company, 1994.

Allen Kurta. *Mammals of the Great Lakes Region*. Ann Arbor, Mich.: University of Michigan Press, 1995.

Chris Stall. *Animal Tracks of the Great Lakes States*. Seattle, Wash.: Mountaineers Books, 1990.

Michele Strutin. *The Smithsonian Guides to Natural America: The Great Lakes*. Washington, D.C.: Smithsonian Books, 1996.

Helen H. Tanner, ed. *Atlas of Great Lakes Indian History*. Norman, Okla.: University of Oklahoma Press, 1987.

Special Thanks

In creating this fifth anthology in the *Stories from Where We Live* series, I relied first and foremost on the authors whose works grace these pages. My heartfelt thanks go out to each of them for helping to celebrate the Great Lakes region with their well-crafted words, and for generously sharing these selections with our readers.

As always, I received able assistance from my team of keen-eyed, kind-hearted readers: Priscilla Howell, Jen Kretser, Jen Lindstrom, Miriam Stewart, and Robin Kelsey. Greg Larson took over as my manuscript reader at Milkweed and offered many thoughtful insights. The librarians in the local history department of the Niagara Falls Public Library delivered a helpful packet of information about ice bridges and other Niagara Falls events. Gary Paul Nabhan put me on the trail of some excellent writing from Indiana. April Pulley Sayre reviewed the introduction and appendixes for ecological accuracy, and David Jude assisted us with our diagram of lake zones.

Because I grew up in Michigan, editing this anthology was a kind of homecoming, reminding me of the many people who nurtured my appreciation of both literature and nature throughout my early life. Among these are the many fine English teachers who encouraged my love of reading and writing during my tenure in the Ann Arbor public schools, most notably Phil Rusten, Lori Gravelyn, and David Stringer. In addition, Lois Theis led my sixth grade class from Park Washtenaw to Point Pelee National Park to enrich our understanding of the natural world. With her I identified my first skunk cabbage, created my first nature journal, and ate my first granola bar. Phil Rusten, too, shared his love of the Michigan outdoors through the example of his nature writing and photography, and through his choice of reading and writing assignments. I am especially grateful for his instruction in the art of playing hooky on a beautiful spring day.

Outside of the classroom, many individuals shared in my discovery of the natural world. Gail Hawker organized thrilling canoe trips, cross-country ski adventures, and trips to Warren Dunes. With the Knott family, I enjoyed many fine days in wild and semiwild places, from the marshes of Joslin Lake to the islands of Temagami, Ontario. And with the Kelsey-Cone-Miller clan, I learned why paddling the blue lakes of the Quetico is such a time-honored family tradition.

Last but not least, I don't think I would ever have become so fond of Michigan without the many hours spent romping and roaming with Jenny Ause, Beth Hackman, Lee Ann Jackson, Anne Knott, and Lisa Lindquist. They made me laugh, think, and appreciate the blessings of friends at a time when whole afternoons could still be spent sitting in an Arboretum tree. And although we are no longer so free nor so proximate, they still do.

Contributor Acknowledgments

Ellen Airgood, "At Uglyfish Lake." Copyright © 2003 by Ellen Airgood. Printed with permission from the author.

Day Alexander, "Neengay, the Story Giver." Copyright © 2003 by Day Alexander. Printed with permission from the author.

Robert Alexander, "Weekend," in *White Pine Sucker River: Poems* 1970–1990 (Minneapolis: New Rivers Press, 1993), 13. Copyright © 1993 by Robert Alexander. Reprinted with permission from the author.

Laurie Allmann, "Gems in the Jack Pine," originally published as "Huron National Forest" in *Far from Tame: Reflections from the Heart of a Continent* (Minneapolis: University of Minnesota Press, 1996), 69–73. Copyright © 1996 by Laurie Allmann. Reprinted with permission from the author.

Margaret Atwood, "Apple Jelly," from "Daybooks II" in *Selected Poems 1966–1984* (Toronto: Oxford University Press, 1990), 240. Copyright © 1978, 1990 by Margaret Atwood. Reprinted with permission from Oxford University Press Canada and the author.

Jill Barrie, "Crows," *Yankee Magazine* (September 1998): 32. Copyright © 1998 by Jill Barrie. Reprinted with permission from the author.

Jack Becklund, "A Bear in the Backyard," excerpted from *Summers with the Bears: Six Seasons in the Minnesota Woods* (New York: Hyperion, 1999), 116–18. Copyright © 1999 by Jack Becklund. Reprinted with permission from Hyperion.

Louis W. Campbell with Claire Gavin, "Shorthand on the Snow," excerpted from *The Marshes of Southwestern Lake Erie* (Athens: Ohio University Press, 1995), 10–13. Copyright © 1995 by Louis W. Campbell. Reprinted with permission from Ohio University Press.

Mary Bartlett Caskey, "An Evening on Isle Royale," *Snowy Egret* 64, no. 1 (Spring 2001): 34. Copyright © 2001 by Mary Bartlett Caskey. Reprinted with permission from the author.

Bruce Catton, "Winter Season," excerpted from *Waiting for the Morning Train: An American Boyhood* (Garden City: Doubleday, 1972), 58, 60–61. Copyright © 1972 by Bruce Catton. Reprinted with permission from Doubleday, a division of Random House, Inc.

Sandra Cisneros, "Four Skinny Trees," in *The House on Mango Street* (New York: Vintage Books, 1991), 74–75. Copyright © 1984 by Sandra Cisneros. Reprinted with permission from Susan Bergholz Literary Services, New York.

Ann Cooper, "Beaver Rendezvous." Copyright © 2003 by Ann Cooper. Printed with permission from the author.

Ellen Creager, "The Ice Deer." Copyright © 2003 by Ellen Creager. Printed with permission from the author.

Marjorie Carlson Davis, "A Flash of Gold." Copyright © 2003 by Marjorie Carlson Davis. Printed with permission from the author.

Carol Farley, "Christmas Tree Miracle." Copyright © 2003 by Carol Farley. Printed with permission from the author.

Antwone Quenton Fisher, "Rain," excerpted from *Finding Fish: A Memoir* (New York: William Morrow, 2001), 98–99. Copyright © 2001 by Antwone Quenton Fisher and Mim Eichler Rivas. Reprinted with permission from HarperCollins Publishers, Inc.

Phyllis I. Harris, "A Clutch of Flowers," *Intersections* (Illinois Wesleyan University Writer's Conference, 1990). Copyright © 1990 by Phyllis I. Harris. Reprinted with permission from the author.

Gwen Hart, "Miracle," *Acorn Whistle* 3, no. 1 (Spring 1999): 36. Copyright © 1999 by Gwen Hart. Reprinted with permission from the author.

Marie Howe, "The Copper Beech," in *What the Living Do* (New York: W. W. Norton, 1998), 34. Copyright © 1998 by Marie Howe. Reprinted with permission from W. W. Norton and Company, Inc.

Louis Jenkins, "Return Portage," in *An Almost Human Gesture* (St. Paul, Minn.: Eighties Press, 1987), 37. Copyright © 1987 by Louis Jenkins. Reprinted with permission from the author.

Pat Kertzman, "The Raccoon Brigade," *Cricket* 26, no. 9 (May 1999): 44–48. Copyright © 1999 by Patricia A. Kertzman. Reprinted with permission from the author.

David Kline, "Hay Field Bestiary," in *Scratching the Woodchuck: Nature on an Amish Farm* (Athens: University of Georgia Press, 1997), 67–69. Copyright © 1997 by David Kline. Reprinted with permission from the University of Georgia Press.

John Knott, "Serious Fishing," in *The Huron River: Voices from the Watershed,* ed. John Knott and Keith Taylor (Ann Arbor: University of Michigan Press, 2000), 178–80. Copyright © 2000 by the University of Michigan. Reprinted with permission from the University of Michigan Press.

Aldo Leopold, "A Mighty Fortress," in *A Sand County Almanac and Sketches Here and There* (New York: Oxford University Press, 1949), 73–77. Copyright © 1949, 1977 by Oxford University Press. Reprinted with permission from Oxford University Press, Inc.

Marcia Lipson, "Prairie after Rain." Copyright © 2003 by Marcia Lipson. Printed with permission from the author's estate.

Laura Lush, "The Worm Girl," in *Hometown* (Montreal: Vehicule Press, 1991), 30. Copyright © 1991 by Laura Lush. Reprinted with permission from the author.

JoAnn Early Macken, "We Are the Early Risers." Copyright © 2003 by JoAnn Early Macken. Printed with permission from the author.

Freya Manfred, "The Glowing Brown Snails of Blueberry Lake," *North Coast Review,* no. 19 (2001): 11. Copyright © 2001 by Freya Manfred. Reprinted with permission from the author.

Charles E. Misner, "Adrift on Niagara," in *Anthology and Bibliography of Niagara Falls, Vol. I,* by Charles Mason Dow (Albany: State of New York, J.B. Lyon Company, Printers: 1921), 402–5. Originally appeared as "My experience on the great ice bridge in the gorge of the Niagara river at Niagara Falls, January 22, 1899," *Home* 12 (March 1899): 239–42.

Don Moser, "Evening Flight," in *McDougal and Littel Literature: Blue Level,* ed. David W. Foote and Brenda Perkins (Evanston, Ill.: McDougal and Littel, 1984), 184–90. Copyright © 1957 by *Harper's Magazine.* Reprinted with permission from the author.

Sigurd F. Olson, "Moon Magic," in *The Singing Wilderness* (New York: Alfred A. Knopf, 1956), 84–89. Copyright © 1956 by Sigurd F. Olson. Reprinted with permission from Alfred A. Knopf, a division of Random House, Inc.

Julie Parson-Nesbitt, "Milwaukee River Poem." Copyright © 2003 by Julie Parson-Nesbitt. Printed with permission from the author.

Roger Pfingston, "Journal Entry: Lake Michigan, July," *WordWrights,* no. 17 (Fall 1999–Winter 2000): 37. Copyright © 1999 by Roger Pfingston. Reprinted with permission from the author.

Susan Power, "Chicago Waters," excerpted from *Roofwalker* (Minneapolis: Milkweed Editions, 2002), 190–99. Copyright © 2002 by Susan Power. Reprinted with permission from the author.

Katharine Crawford Robey, "Fireworks!" *Cricket* 19, no. 11 (July 1992): 10–16. Copyright © 1992 by Katharine Crawford Robey. Reprinted with permission from the author. "Great Northern Pike." Copyright © 2003 by Katharine Crawford Robey. Printed with permission from the author.

William Pitt Root, "From the Cellar." Copyright © 2003 by William Pitt Root. Printed with permission from the author.

Sara St. Antoine, "Leaves." Copyright © 2003 by Sara St. Antoine. Printed with permission from the author.

April Pulley Sayre, "Fairies' Washing." Copyright © 2003 by April Pulley Sayre. Printed with permission from the author.

Shannon Sexton, "Summer at Silver Creek Farm." Copyright © 2003 by Shannon Sexton. Printed with permission from the author.

Raymond Souster, "Snowy Morning with Squirrels," in *Collected Poems of Raymond Souster, Volume Eight, 1991–1993* (Ottawa: Oberon Press, 1999), 119. Copyright © 1999 by Raymond Souster. Reprinted with permission from Oberon Press.

Gene Stratton-Porter, "The Gold Medal Flower," excerpted from *Tales You Won't Believe* (Garden City: Doubleday, Page, 1926), 79–82.

Edwin Way Teale, "The Box Camera," in *Dune Boy: The Early Years of a Naturalist* (New York: Dodd, Mead, 1943), 229–34. Copyright © 1943 by Edwin Way Teale. Reprinted with permission from the University of Connecticut.

Pamela Uschuk, "Hummingbird," in *Without Birds, Without Flowers, Without Trees* (Chico, Calif.: Flume Press, 1991), 18. Copyright © 1991 by Pamela Uschuk. Reprinted with permission from the author.

George Vukelich, "The Turtle," *Cricket* 25, no. 11 (July 1998): 30–33. First published in *University of Kansas City Review* (1959.) Copyright © 1959 by George Vukelich. Reprinted with permission from Helen Vukelich.

Lisa Wheeler, "Mush Again." Copyright © 2003 by Lisa Wheeler. Printed with permission from the author.

Gretchen Woelfle, "Saving Lake Erie." Copyright © 2003 by Gretchen Woelfle. Printed with permission from the author.

Abe Louise Young, "First Night of Summer in Chicago." Copyright © 2003 by Abe Louise Young. Printed with permission from the author.

About the Editor

Sara St. Antoine grew up in Ann Arbor, Michigan. She holds a bachelor's degree in English from Williams College and a master's degree in Environmental Studies from the Yale School of Forestry and Environmental Studies. Currently living in Cambridge, Massachusetts, she enjoys walking along the Charles River and seeing black-crowned night herons hunkered in the trees.

About the Illustrators

Paul Mirocha is a designer and illustrator of books about nature for children and adults. His first book, *Gathering the Desert,* by Gary Paul Nabhan, won the 1985 John Burroughs Medal for natural history. He lives in Tucson, Arizona, with his daughters, Anna and Claire.

Trudy Nicholson is an illustrator of nature with a background in medical and scientific illustration. She received her B.S. in Fine Arts at Columbia University and has worked as a natural-science illustrator in a variety of scientific fields for many years. She lives in Cabin John, Maryland.

The World As Home, the nonfiction publishing program of Milkweed Editions, is dedicated to exploring our relationship to the natural world. Not espousing any particular environmentalist or political agenda, these books are a forum for distinctive literary writing that not only alerts the reader to vital issues but offers personal testimonies to living harmoniously with other species in urban, rural, and wilderness communities.

Milkweed Editions publishes with the intention of making a humane impact on society, in the belief that literature is a transformative art uniquely able to convey the essential experiences of the human heart and spirit. To that end, Milkweed publishes distinctive voices of literary merit in handsomely designed, visually dynamic books, exploring the ethical, cultural, and esthetic issues that free societies need continually to address. Milkweed Editions is a not-for-profit press.

For more information on other books published by Milkweed Editions for intermediate readers, contact Milkweed at (800) 520-6455 or visit our website (www.milkweed.org).

Books for Middle-Grade Readers
by Milkweed Editions

Tides by V. M. Caldwell

The Ocean Within by V. M. Caldwell

Alligator Crossing by Marjorie Stoneman Douglas

The Monkey Thief by Aileen Kilgore Henderson

Treasure of Panther Peak by Aileen Kilgore Henderson

The Dog with Golden Eyes by Frances Wilbur

Join Us

Since its genesis as *Milkweed Chronicle* in 1979, Milkweed has helped hundreds of emerging writers reach their readers. Thanks to the generosity of foundations and of individuals like you, Milkweed Editions is able to continue its nonprofit mission of publishing books chosen on the basis of literary merit—the effect they have on the human heart and spirit—rather than on the basis of how they impact the bottom line. That's a miracle our readers have made possible.

In addition to purchasing Milkweed books, you can join the growing community of Milkweed supporters. Individual contributions of any amount are both meaningful and welcome. Contact us for a Milkweed catalog or log on to www.milkweed.org and click on "About Milkweed," then "Supporting Milkweed," to find out about our donor program, or simply call (800) 520-6455 and ask about becoming one of Milkweed's contributors. As a nonprofit press, Milkweed belongs to you, the community. Milkweed's board, its staff, and especially the authors whose careers you help launch thank you for reading our books and supporting our mission in any way you can.

Interior design by Wendy Holdman.
The text is typeset in 12/16 point Legacy Book
by Stanton Publication Services, Inc.
Printed on acid-free 50# Fraser Trade Book paper
by Friesen Corporation.

NORTHWEST

PACIFIC

COAST

ROCKY MOUNTAINS

TH

BOREA

GREAT

NORT

CALIFORNIA

COAST

WESTERN

DESERTS

AND

PLATEAUS

HAWAIIAN

ISLANDS